1220 Days

The story of U.S. Marine Edmond Babler and his experiences in Japanese Prisoner of War Camps during World War II.
Second Edition

Robert C. Daniels

authorHOUSE®

AuthorHouse™
1663 Liberty Drive
Bloomington, IN 47403
www.authorhouse.com
Phone: 1-800-839-8640

Second edition © Copyright 2011, Robert C. Daniels
Original © Copyright 2004, Robert C. Daniels
All rights reserved.

No part of this book may be reproduced, stored in a retrieval system, or transmitted by any means without the written permission of the author.

First published by AuthorHouse 10/31/2011

ISBN: 978-1-4670-5427-0 (sc)
ISBN: 978-1-4670-5428-7 (hc)
ISBN: 978-1-4670-5429-4 (e)

Library of Congress Control Number: 2011918361

Printed in the United States of America

Any people depicted in stock imagery provided by Thinkstock are models, and such images are being used for illustrative purposes only. Certain stock imagery © Thinkstock.

Because of the dynamic nature of the Internet, any web addresses or links contained in this book may have changed since publication and may no longer be valid. The views expressed in this work are solely those of the author and do not necessarily reflect the views of the publisher, and the publisher hereby disclaims any responsibility for them.

Dedication

This book is dedicated to all the men who served our country so faithfully in the Philippine battlefields on Bataan and Corregidor, and suffered and endured the tortures of a living hell in the prison camps.

Acknowledgments

In writing this account I owe a personal debt of gratitude to several people. First there is my wife Rebecca who not only stuck by me throughout the long days and nights of research, writing, and rewriting, but who also gave me constant encouragement.

In addition, the completion of this book would not have been possible without the help of Jeanette Babler. I am deeply indebted to her for her efforts in answering my seemingly unending string of questions and providing me with not only a copy Ed's original memoirs, but countless family pictures, newspaper clippings, and corroborating information from Ed's friends and fellow former POWs. I am also greatly indebted to Jeannette for her superb editing qualities.

I am also indebted to both Andrew Baggs, PhD. and my very good friend Jesse Tate, who read my drafts and gave me valuable insight into my writing techniques. I also wish to thank Robert V. Aquilina, the Assistant Head, Reference Section, History and Museums Division of the Marine Corps Historical Society in Washington, D.C. who graciously supplied me with the materials at his disposal. And John Patrick Zimba, a former member of the Second Battalion, 4th Marine Regiment who also went into captivity on Corregidor and who graciously allowed me to interview him, gaining valuable insight into both the Battle of Corregidor and the interment in Japanese prisoner of war camps.

Table of Contents

Dedication	v
Acknowledgments	vii
Preface to the Second Edition	xi
Forward	xiii
Prologue	xix
1 From Wisconsin to the Philippines	1
2 The War Begins	17
3 Into Captivity – Cabanatuan - Philippines	31
4 Palawan and McKinley Field – Philippines	45
5 Nielsen Field – Philippines	59
6 Zeblon Field – Philippines	77
7 Hell Ship - From the Philippines to Japan	87
8 Mining Coal in Japan	97
9 Surviving in Japan	111
10 Senso Wari – Our Captivity Ends	125
Epilogue	141
About the Author	145
Selected Bibliography	147
Notes	149
Index	153

Preface to the Second Edition

After the first printing, Jeanette Babler, Ed's widow, pointed out to me that the actual writing of his memoirs seemed to help relieve Ed's sometimes nearly overwhelming tensions that would build up upon remembering his ordeal, even decades after it ended. She conveyed to me that he would sometimes write portions of these memoirs after recalling upsetting memories; at other times he would just sit and write, recalling the memories as he did so. Usually, as she stated, he did so in a very upset manner, but his writing would always seem to calm him down.

Although very therapeutic in nature for Ed, this also resulted in many of his sentences being of nearly bullet type in format with various subjects sometimes intermingling. Some of these were in order, some were scattered over several pages: a sentence here, another there, and yet another several paragraphs or even pages later. This made it somewhat difficult to properly put the items into correct context and order, especially since Ed had passed away several years before my writing of this book and was not available for consultation.

As I alluded to at the end of the Forward in the original printing (which remains intact in this second edition), in formatting this edition I fully attempted to maintain Ed's story, whenever possible, using Ed's own words when I could adequately place them in proper sentence structure with little or no grammatical change. When I could not, I took the liberty to reword them, but took great strides to insure that the context remained in tact. In addition, since it was and remains Ed's story, I chose to write in the first person format.

In this second edition, in an attempt to do a better service to Ed and his fellow POWs, I have incorporated several minor typographical, punctuation, and grammatical error changes that were discovered after the initial printing. I have also chosen to change from using content footnotes for the insertion of clarification and corroborating information to incorporating these into the text in the form of encapsulated brackets where deemed necessary to give the reader a better understanding of the overall picture of the war in relation to what Ed was experiencing. In some instances I have also expanded upon some of this clarification and corroborating information. The remaining footnotes have been changed to endnotes and contain, for the most part, only reference material. I feel this will make for a smother flow for the reader.

In addition, since the original printing it has come to my attention that two POW camps in the Japanese home islands were both referred to as the or an *Omine* camp, which has led to some confusion, even for those who actually lived at the camps. Ed repeatedly used the name Omine Machi in his memoirs when referring to the camp that he was incarcerated in while in Japan. Therefore, in the initial printing I indicated that he was at the Omine-machi camp, which I related to as the Hiroshima #6 camp on the Island of Honshu. However, in gaining access to some of the various camp rosters, it was discovered that Ed was actually in the Fukuoka Camp 05B-Omine on the Island of Kyushu. For this mistake, I humbly apologize and have made the appropriate corrections properly referencing the Fukuoka Camp in the applicable map that I include within these pages. All other content in this second edition remains the same as the original printing, with the exception of the already noted minor editing corrections.

In writing this book, I hope that I have done an adequate job that does justice to not only Ed, but to all of those who suffered throughout such an ordeal. I believe that the result is, at the very least, close to what Ed had endured and the timeline that he endured it, and that he would be pleased with what's written in these pages. With this said, any incorrect statements, miss-quotes, or misspellings of personal or place names remains solely my responsibility, and I sincerely apologize in advance for any errors.

Robert C. Daniels

Forward

The surprise attack on Pearl Harbor, Hawaii, on 7 December 1941 suddenly thrust the United States into the Second World War, a war that would last for nearly four years and cost the lives of 407,316 Americans while wounding another 671,846. Each year on the anniversary of the surprise attack Pearl Harbor is reverently recalled, and rightly so—it was a bitter surprise attack on American soil, against Americans. Subsequently, much has been published about this attack in both book and film format.

However, few Americans are aware that had it not been for bad weather over the Island of Formosa, Japanese Admiral Chichi Nagumo's Pearl Harbor naval strike force may not have been the first to attack Americans on 7 December 1941. "Remember Pearl Harbor" may not have been the rallying call for many Americans flocking to recruiting stations soon afterward. The attack on Pearl Harbor was just a part of the Japanese offensive planned for 7 December. The overall plan called for simultaneous attacks not only on Pearl Harbor, but on several other American and Allied locations in the Pacific as well.

One of these additional locations was the American Protectorate of the Philippine Islands where only a weather front over Formosa kept the Japanese from launching their planned massive air strike against the Philippines as scheduled—at the exact time Nagumo's forces were to attack Pearl Harbor. Although the weather front only delayed the air strike a few hours, it was enough to keep the Philippines from being the first major objective to be attacked on 7 December 1941, and, in the annuals of history, help ensure that its attack was overshadowed by the attack at Pearl Harbor.

While much has been published about Pearl Harbor and World War II in general, little of what has been published relates to the desperate fight for survival the American and Filipino forces endured during the hours, days, and months following the Pearl Harbor attack. Nonetheless, the attack on the Philippines was just as overwhelming to its defenders as to those who defended Pearl Harbor; possibly even more so.

On 7 December 1941 the American-Filipino forces in the Philippines, led by General Douglas MacArthur, consisted of 16,000 American troops, 150 aircraft, 16 surface ships, and 29 submarines. Added to this was the 60,000 fledgling and under trained Philippine Army, of which, in reality, only the 12,000 man American-trained Philippine Scouts Division was actually combat-ready. The other ten Philippine divisions were still effectively in training and not yet fit to fight.[1]

Of the American forces in the Philippines very few were actual combat troops; most being aircrew, mechanics, artillery, and support staff. Although at the outbreak of the war MacArthur had at his disposal the largest concentration of B-17 bombers in the United States arsenal, like at Hawaii, nearly all of the combat aircraft stationed in the Philippines were destroyed in the first wave of Japanese air strikes. This air strike, occurring at approximately 12 noon on 8 December, roughly eight and a half hours after the attack on Pearl Harbor, left the Japanese in nearly unopposed command of the air.

General Masaharu Homma, the commander of the Japanese invasion force attacking the Philippine Islands, began landing his troops on the main Philippine Island of Luzon on 10 December 1941 and launched his advance towards Manila, the Philippine capital. Soon afterwards, Homma landed additional troops on the southeastern portion of Luzon and, after bringing his main landing force ashore north of the capital on 21 December and still another force ashore west of the capital on 24 December, forced MacArthur's American and Filipino troops to fall back onto the Bataan Peninsula and the offshore island fortress of Corregidor. Nearly overnight the Bataan Peninsula, roughly thirty miles long by fifteen miles wide at its widest, swelled with an estimated 83,000 American and Filipino troops and 26,000 Filipino civilian refugees.[2]

In actuality, the American strategic plan for the defense of the Philippines in the case of a Japanese invasion called for such a move. Known as the Orange Plan, this strategic plan had been devised and studied by students at the United States War College ever since 1926. The plan called for the abandonment of the Philippine capital and the withdrawal of all American and Filipino forces to the Bataan Peninsula, which, with its thick jungle and rocky volcanic terrain and with the proper amount of supplies and pre-invasion preparations, made for an ideal defensive position. The plan called for supplies to be strategically located throughout the peninsula and defensive positions to be pre-built. If properly supplied and fortified as such, it was thought that the American and Filipino forces could defend this peninsula, protected from the sea by the offshore fortresses of Corregidor, Frank, Drum, and Hughes, for up to six months until the United States Navy could fight its way to the relief of the Philippine defenders.

The Orange Plan itself was a sound plan, and never during the invasion were General Homma's troops superior in number to MacArthur's. But, from the beginning, things went wrong for the American and Filipino forces. MacArthur steadfastly believed that the Japanese would not attack any sooner than April 1942, and it was to this timeframe that MacArthur geared his troop training and war preparation program. As a result, when Homma's troops landed on Luzon in December 1941, the 60,000 strong Filipino Army was made up of, for the most part, raw, untrained troops—many having never even fired a weapon. To compound matters, MacArthur, refusing to abandon Manila, abandoned the Orange Plan instead, ordered his supplies scattered around the capital and other strategic defensive points on Luzon, and sent his ill-trained Filipino Army to stall the Japanese advance. To this end, the hastily organized and ill-trained Filipino defenders, although many fighting bravely, were quickly overwhelmed by Homma's well trained and battle seasoned troops.

By the time MacArthur finally decided to revert back to the Orange Plan, his supply corps, although desperately attempting to move tons of food, ammunition, fuel, and medical supplies to the Bataan Peninsula, were hampered by air raids, lack of vehicles, lack of personnel, and, most importantly, lack of time. As a result, they were only able to relocate a portion of the much needed supplies to the peninsula. In addition, the pre-invasion construction of the planned Bataan fortified defensive positions had also been neglected. The effects of MacArthur's failure to quickly implement the Orange Plan soon became evident when, with the arrival of approximately 100,000 additional people on the Bataan Peninsula, rations soon ran short and few, if any, defensible positions were available.

Help, promised from Washington, was not only hoped for, but expected by both the American and Filipino forces. However, senior military and government personnel knew otherwise. President Franklin Delano Roosevelt had, as recently as June 1941, signed the secret "European first strategy" pact with British Prime Minister Winston Churchill. This pact, which was turned into War Plan 5, committed the United States forces to defeating the Axis Powers in Europe first, while fighting a defensive war in the Pacific. Unbeknownst to the American and Filipino forces on Bataan and the offshore coastal garrisons of Corregidor and her sister fortress islands, War Plan 5 doomed the defenders to either annihilation, starvation, or surrender. A lucky few, including General Douglas MacArthur, would be evacuated. The others would be sacrificed.

Estimates vary, but due to dwindling supplies on Bataan, on 8 April 1942 General Edward King was forced to surrender nearly 70,000 men, including 12,000 Americans, to General Homma's forces. Many of these were sick or wounded; all were near the starvation level due to the severe shortage of rations. These prisoners were marched into captivity on what became known as the infamous "Bataan Death March." Again, estimates vary, however, between 16,000 and 25,000 Americans and Filipinos died on this march due to the Japanese open brutality towards their captives. Many of the prisoners, who were already nearly emaciated by the time they surrendered, died of sickness and fatigue along the way; others succumbed from wounds received during the battle of Bataan. Still others were beaten to death or outright executed by bayoneting, shooting, or beheading by the Japanese. Approximately 2,300 of those that died or were killed during this march were Americans.

On 6 May 1942, after sustaining shelling for twenty-seven straight days and feverishly attempting to fend off an invasion, the forces on Corregidor, under General Jonathan Wainwright, surrendered, leaving the Philippine Islands entirely in Japanese hands and adding roughly another 14,000 American and Filipino troops to the rolls of Japanese held POWs. United States Marine Corporal Edmond Babler and his fellow 4th Marine Regiment, the "Chinese Marines," were among these additional American and Filipino forces forced to surrender on Corregidor.

What follows is a compilation of Ed's memoirs of the period that he appropriately entitled *1220 Days In Hell*, and is Ed's story from the time he joined the Marine Corps on 20 December 1938 until his return from 1,220 days of captivity in Japanese prisoner of war camps. It is intended, in Ed's own words, as "A true history of my struggle for survival in Japanese Prison Camps in the jungles of the Philippine Islands, on air-fields and a coal mine in Japan."

Written in the first person and, wherever possible, using Ed's own words, I have taken great strides to maintain the contents of Ed's memoirs in its original context. With this in mind, I have chosen to record, with only a few exceptions, the Japanese words and phrases contained herein in the phonetic form in which Ed originally wrote them; the way he remembered them.

A corporal when captured, Ed writes of what he saw, knew, experienced, and remembered as a Marine of that rank during his tour in Shanghai, China, the battle for the Philippines, and his 1,220 days in brutal Japanese captivity. It is his views and memories, with no apologies made nor intended to conform to the modern concept of political correctness. I have sparingly inserted clarifications and corroborating information in encapsulated brackets where deemed necessary to give the reader a better understanding of the 'overall picture' of the war in relation to what Ed was experiencing. For the most part, facts, figures, and dates are only referenced when obtained from single source material.

Robert C. Daniels

Prologue

One of Ferdinand and Katherine (Goetz) Babler's seven children, Edmond Joseph Babler was born at the Babler family home on 14 December 1913 in the small rural Wisconsin town of Maplewood, located in Door County in the east-central part of the state. After graduating from Brussels High School, Ed spent several years working in his father's blacksmith shop, which specialized in horse shoeing and wagon and buggy building, and on the two family farms. Ed also spent six months working in the Civilian Conservation Corps (CCC) camp at Star Lake, Wisconsin, and another six months at the CCC camp at Blue Lake, Wisconsin.

Ed had always been an enthusiastic wrestler and boxer, and competed in approximately thirty fights at state fairs and Golden Glove tournaments throughout Wisconsin and the Upper Peninsula of Michigan. He also accompanied two of his cousins on a trip riding the rails from Wisconsin to California and back. While on this trip he won several boxing matches in San Diego, California.

It was in late 1938, at age twenty-five, when Ed decided to join the Marine Corps. This is his story, from his entry and training in the Marine Corps, his garrison duty in Shanghai, China, his participation in the battle of the Philippine Islands, and his daily fight for survival as a prisoner of war at the hands of his Japanese captors.

Map 1: Western Pacific Ocean

1 From Wisconsin to the Philippines

December of 1938 saw the depression at its peak. I wasn't going anywhere as a boxer, having just lost my last two fights, and, in reality, the $30 worth of boxing purses I made every month or so just wasn't enough. So, although I hated to leave home just before Christmas, I enlisted in the United States Marine Corps in Chicago, Illinois, on 20 December 1938. I recall the recruiting sergeant telling me that anything could happen during my tour of duty, including a war. Nonetheless, I told him that I was ready to go.

I traveled by rail to San Diego, California, where I went through a rough eight-week training period, followed by two weeks on the rifle range at La Jolla, California. Upon completion of these ten weeks of training I was assigned to B Company, 1st Battalion Fleet Marine Force, Sixth Marine Force, which was stationed at La Jolla.

At that time Shanghai, China, had the reputation of being the best liberty town in the Marine Corps, and it seemed as if every Marine wanted to spend at least part of his enlistment there, and I was no exception. However, being a junior Marine with only a few months in the Corps, I had to do some real dealing to get my name on the list. The battalion football coach made a verbal agreement with me saying that if I would practice with his football team, he would insure my name was added to the Shanghai list. So I began attending football practices.

Besides working out with the football team, I also trained four nights a week with the pros at the Gold Street Gym in downtown La Jolla. Between the football practice and the boxing training, I was able to keep myself in top physical shape, which helped enable me to defeat all of the local heavyweights in nine amateur boxing bouts at the Coliseum in San Diego. I continued boxing and, as promised, practicing with the football team until 13 November 1939 when I departed for Shanghai on the transport *Henderson*. Major Hall had indeed placed my name on the list. [The *Henderson* was a transport that routinely made stops in both Shanghai and the Philippine capital of Manila.]

One of my first Marine Corps excitements happened the day before the *Henderson* left. I was part of the detail assigned to load supplies onto the transport, which was moored about twelve feet from a dock at the Mare Island Navy Base. While carrying quarters of beef across the gangplank to the hold, the man I was working with became careless and allowed the side of beef we were carrying to hit the side of the ship, which in turn caused me to be knocked overboard. I can recall hearing the duty boatswain calling out, "Man overboard," as I fell towards the cold water. I sank down to about what seemed like forty feet of water before finally being able to begin my upward swim. When I finally surfaced a sailor tossed me a life jacket and several men pulled me to the dock. As soon as I walked aboard the ship I was wrapped in several blankets and handed hot coffee. Even with blankets and the coffee, it took several minutes for the chill to disappear.

The next day at 12:00 noon, with me warm and dry onboard and with only 25¢ in my pocket, which I soon spent having my shoes re-heeled, the *Henderson* departed San Diego heading towards Honolulu, Hawaii. For many of the young men onboard, both Marines and sailors alike, the trip was the first Pacific Ocean crossing they made onboard a transport. With the ship constantly swaying from side to side in the high seas, coupled with water splashing onto the main deck when the sea became really rough, many of the men soon became seasick.

Onboard the *Henderson* was the Navy's runner-up to the Pacific Fleet heavyweight boxing champion. Once the word was out that I had fought at San Diego the ship's crew wanted me to fight their Navy runner-up, so a smoker match was arranged, which turned out to be the highlight of my voyage across the Pacific.

My opponent was a member of the whale boat crew and had large, well developed shoulders. A Navy chief [Chief Petty Officer] was chosen to be the referee, and his orders to us just before the fight were simple; "After the bell, come out, touch gloves and begin fighting." Upon hearing the bell sound, I did just that—or at least I tried to. As soon as I put my hands out to touch gloves, my opponent let fly a wild right roundhouse, which I managed to avoid with a quick duck. I decided right then and there that I was going to punish this sailor for his attempt at hitting me with that sucker punch. Boring in, I hit him with everything but the ring post and the water bucket. As I battered him from one side of the ring to the other he reeled around in seemingly desperate attempts to hang on. It doesn't take long with this type of boxing before a fight turns into a rough and tumble brawl, and ours did just that. Both of us abandoned formal boxing altogether and just began slugging it out toe to toe, and the ref didn't make much of an effort to stop us.

The ocean that night was particularly rough, which caused the ship and, consequently, the two of us to sway from one side to the other, which only added to the fray. Although the big sailor repeatedly fell into the ropes, the referee continued to enable him to stay on his feet, so my opponent was able to stay up and keep reeling around again and again. If only he would have stood up and fought I'm sure I would have been able to knock him out that night. Nonetheless, even though I wasn't able to chalk up a knockout against him, I was finally declared the winner of the fight. This meant the Marines had beaten the Navy, a fact that hadn't escaped the attention of the Marine Corps brass that was sailing with us.

I knew the rivalry between the Navy and Marine Corps was legendary, and my winning this fight had meant a lot for the Marines onboard. This fact was made apparent to me one night later in the voyage. The wind became very cold as we approached China, especially at night. And while I was standing guard duty on one of those frigid nights, because of the cold, I was unable to properly salute a Marine lieutenant as he passed by. It was when he simply replied, "That's OK Babler," that I knew just how seriously the Marine Corps brass took this rivalry, and my defeating the Navy's runner-up heavyweight champion, the Navy's pride and joy, had made this same Marine Corps brass very happy.

On 10 December 1939 the *Henderson* tied up at the Bund, which was located adjacent to Nanking Road and about eight blocks from downtown Shanghai. We marched off the ship and onto the waiting motor transport trucks for the ride to our quarters, which turned out to be large apartment houses leased from the Chinese.

I had never before seen such large crowds of people in one area as I did on the streets of Shanghai as we passed them by on the way to our quarters. At the time, Shanghai was a city of about seven million inhabitants, and thousands of its Chinese citizens were milling around like cattle. It was then that I truly realized that my stay in Shanghai would indeed be a very exciting and interesting one.

During my tour in Shanghai I was assigned to B Company, 1st Battalion of the 4th Marine Regiment, which was billeted on Ferry Road. Our daily routine was similar to that of a rifle company in the States, although we pulled more guard duty. This guard duty consisted mainly of manning one of the dozen or so guard posts throughout the American sector, each of which were manned twenty-four hours a day.

[In 1941, the City of Shanghai contained many foreign nationals, several of which maintained their own settlements. Included among these were the United States, Russia, England, Italy, Japan, and France. Due to the nearly constant turmoil throughout war-torn China, these nations maintained armed contingents in Shanghai to protect their nation's interests. The 4th Marine Regiment, known as the "China Marines," had been stationed in Shanghai since 1926 to protect the American interests. Ever since the outbreak of war in Europe, the international settlements in Shanghai had been deteriorating. In addition, from across the Soochow Creek, a tributary of the Whangpoo River, the Japanese had been unceasingly attempting to intimidate and undermine the Western powers occupying the various sections of the city.[3]]

When not on duty at one of these posts, our normal day was comprised of an hour of close order drill each morning, with the balance of the day devoted to weapons training, including the rifle, the .45 Colt automatic pistol, and the Browning Automatic Rifle (BAR). This training often consisted of our sergeant breaking down the weapons, placing their parts on our bunks, and then leaving. We were then expected to have the weapons reassembled by the time he returned.

Our mess hall was located two blocks down Ferry Road from our quarters. We always walked these two blocks for our meals, and it was not uncommon along the way to come across cripples and beggars lying in the center of the sidewalk; many whose bodies were covered with sores. A Marine always seemed to be good for a buck or two for these people. Many times, even during the cold winter months when snow covered the ground, we also came across newly born babies wrapped only in newspapers. None of the locals even seemed to care about this.

There were thousands of small shops throughout the city which sold fish, fowl, pork, and vegetables. Many of these shops were similar to our small grocery stores back in the States. However, unlike our small grocery stores, the small shops in Shanghai were open and located along unpaved, dirt streets, and dust and flies covered all the produce. It was no wonder many of the Chinese people died young. It also appeared as though 80 percent of the Shanghai people lived at the poverty level in simple wooden shacks, which were generally connected one to another, allowing little or no privacy.

The city of Shanghai was divided into sectors, with the Americans, English, French, Italians, Russians, and Japanese each controlling a sector. Although I found that the American sector had the best theaters and restaurants, entertainment could be found in the other sectors as well. French Town was my favorite liberty spot because the section was clean, had good restaurants, good theatres, good cabarets, and good-looking girls. The Marine Commandant allowed the men from the other countries into our sector; however, several locations in the sector were considered so dangerous they were placed out of bounds. I was told that in one of these, known as "Blood Alley," you could even get killed. To avoid any serious incidents, these rough areas were well patrolled by the MPs. Nonetheless, I made it a point to stay well enough away from these places.

[It should be noted that, although Ed referred to the senior Marine officer of the regiment as the Commandant, the only Marine holding the title of Commandant is the Commandant of the Marine Corps, the senior General of the Marine Corps. The 4th Marine Regiment's Commanding Officer at the time was Colonel Samuel L. Howard (USMC).[4]]

One of the best features about duty in Shanghai was the rate of exchange, which never fell below seven to one during my twenty-one-month stay there. Many times on paydays the exchange rate went even as high as thirteen to one. We paid Chinese boys to press our uniforms and clean and shine our shoes. They would also do all the household chores for about $1 in gold currency, which we could easily afford.

Not long after my arrival in China I found myself passing many well-dressed American men in downtown Shanghai, all looking as if they were American businessmen. Realizing that there weren't this many American businessmen in Shanghai, I began to think, "Who are all these well-dressed Americans living in Shanghai?" I even saw these same well-dressed Americans drinking expensive whiskey in the Shanghai bars. It wasn't until after about a month of this that I finally noticed that all the men in my company had nice suits and would dress in them when going on liberty. As it turned out, the great exchange rate allowed all the Marines, even privates, plenty of money to spend. All this money enabled my buddies and me to buy tailor-made suits for about $10 apiece in U.S. currency. It also allowed the Marines to drink the usually too expensive whiskey.

The Commandant wanted his men to look neat and sharp at all times, so we always wore our dress uniforms while on guard duty, and since we pulled so much guard duty we ended up wearing our dress uniforms more in Shanghai than we did back in the States. Because of this very few of us would wear uniforms while on liberty, preferring civilian clothes because it felt good to have a change from our norm.

I found that the Chinese were ranked among the best tailors in the world, making wonderful robes containing beautiful dragon designs, bedspreads, tablecloths, and tapestries. I had never seen such excellent quality and handiwork as displayed by these tailors, and I had half a dozen tablecloths and bedspreads made for my mother. I also had robes made for every member of my family, and recall paying only $200 in American currency for the entire purchase. At that time, I was due to return to the States in December 1941 and had full intentions of bringing all these gifts, along with my suit, back with me. But as we'll see later, things didn't turn out that way and none of these items ever made it home.

The Marine Club in Shanghai had the best food, and their beer and whiskey were priced right. It was also open only to the Marines. To get to it we had to walk down the Bubbling Well Road, which was what I would consider to be the main street of Shanghai because it was the entrance to the downtown area and was always clean, well paved, and didn't have any beggars along it.

I well remember the first night the members of my platoon coaxed me into accompanying them to the club. Prior to this outing I was strictly a beer drinker, and not really much of a drinking man at that. Up to this point I had also stayed in my quarters every night and read, eating a candy bar and drinking a coke. But on this night the men of my platoon, many of whom had been in Shanghai for two years or more, decided to get me started and proceeded to furnish me with rum-cokes. It wasn't long before I was drunk, and after I grabbed and flipped over the small table we were sitting around, my buddies put me in a cab and sent me back to our quarters.

Another episode that I'll always remember from my stay there in Shanghai began one night when some Italian Marines came over to our sector for liberty. They went to the Palace Cabaret and were involved in a brawl with a few of our Marines, allegedly beating up our buddies. After a buddy of mine, Don Vidal, and I heard about this, we decided to go dancing at the Palace the next Saturday night and get even. Don was a husky kid from Minneapolis, Minnesota, and a good boxer who trained with me. Neither one of us thought that anyone could whip us in a fight.

After telling several of our buddies about our dancing plans, they decided to go along with us to the Palace. The next Saturday night we indeed found our friends, the Italian Marines, at the Palace. While dancing, Don and I bumped into a few of them and the fight was on. The two of us stood back-to-back and floored six to seven of the Italians. The balance of the remaining Italians then retreated to the tables along the sides of the dance floor and started throwing glasses at us. By that time several of our buddies had also become involved and one of the Italian Marines ended up being hauled over the piano keys. About five minutes later the Shore Patrol arrived. Although I managed to avoid them, Don wasn't as lucky. He had slipped on the floor and got a cut on his hand from the broken glass. He went home with the Shore Patrol.

As it is turned out, though, everyone was happy with the fight and its outcome. The United States Marines had really whipped the Italian Marines and after that night the Italian Marines stayed away for a while, and when they did return they behaved themselves and never bothered any of our Marines again.

[One historian relates that a fight between the American and the Italian Marines had indeed occurred, starting at a local downtown club called the Little Club. The brawl ended up the size of a battalion and sprawled over four of the city's sections, resulting in the deaths of five Italian Marines. As a result, and to prevent additional incidents, both forces were instructed to keep to their own sections of the city. It should be noted that the Italians, in league with Germany, had in June of 1940 declared war on both the British and the French. About the same time, the French Vichy government directed their representatives to cooperate with the Japanese. Both of these resulted in tensions mounting between the various European nationals in the city.[5] In addition, John Patrick Zimba, a fellow 4th Marine, related a similar story in a 3 Feb 2001 personal interview, stating that an Italian officer was thrown down a club stairway. Although the name of the club Ed gives differs from that related to by others, and whether or not both brawls were in fact the same, it is apparent that tensions between the U.S. and Italian Marines in Shanghai was high in 1940, and at least one violent fight ensued.]

Boxing was a very popular sport in Shanghai with a good number of fighters from the United States Marines and Navy, the Russians, the

Chinese, the English, and a few Italians. Being very aggressive and very hard to beat, I found the Russians to be the toughest, roughest, and hardest hitting of all these fighters. Three-fourths of the Russians didn't like boxing as much as just slugging it out, and when we fought them as a team it became more like a Pier Six brawl than a boxing match, with the majority of these fights ending in knockouts.

Our boxing team first fought against the Russians about four months after I arrived in Shanghai. Prior to this match we'd been drinking and dancing a lot and hadn't trained nearly hard enough. Out of eight bouts, I was the only one of us Marines that wasn't stopped. But I too still lost my bout all the same, although I thought I should have won. The Russians, I believe, thought the same way, because they invited me over to their barracks soon afterward where they had drink after drink waiting for me. As fast as I could finish the first drink, the next one was waiting. Not realizing that Vodka was such a powerful drink, I soon found myself having to be escorted back to my quarters by my new Russian friends. The next time I went to visit them I was careful not to accept every drink they offered.

With the loss of this boxing match to the Russians went the loss of a lot of our prestige as well. The 4th Marine Regiment had a wonderful reputation, and we were determined to prove ourselves and win back some of the glory that our predecessors had held for a number of years. This left little doubt that a rematch would take place, and as a result a boxing ring was set up in the quarters of the 2nd Battalion where we began to train hard, sparring every day. Each morning a truck would take the boxing team to the downtown racetrack where we would run six to seven miles. So determined were we to regain the title from the Russians that we restrained from staying out late at nights and nearly completely stopped drinking during this period of training. After four months of this routine we were again in very good shape and challenged the Russians for a rematch.

The Russians knew well that we had been training hard for another match, and they too had been getting ready. I had seen them running through the streets before the morning traffic picked up. On the night of the rematch, which was considered a championship match, the auditorium was packed with United States Marines and sailors, Russians, Chinese, and nearly every sports enthusiast in Shanghai. Both our 4th Marine Regimental Band and the Russian's band were playing, which added to the noise and helped increase the tension throughout the auditorium. No doubt a considerable amount of betting was taking place on the evening's nine scheduled bouts.

At the end of the eighth bout the score was tied and it was my turn to fight. Our trainer, big Jack Taylor, came to me and said, "Ed, it's up to you. We want this fight bad." I replied to Jack that, "I want to win this more than you," and with that I entered the ring determined to do so.

As soon as the bout started I found I was up against a rough and tough slugger who wouldn't stop regardless of how hard or how often I hit him. We met in the center of the ring and just started trading punches. Both of us staggered several times throughout the fight, and although falling against the ropes after taking one of my hits towards the end of the bout, my opponent just would not fall down. It was a long, hard fought fight, but at the end I was finally announced the winner. With my win, the match's final score was five to four in our favor, which meant the United States Marines had retaken the title. We were a happy group of Marines that night. We had come back and proved that we could do it, and once more the 4th Marine Regiment was on top.

After that night the Russians again invited me over for another celebration. Although I was on my guard from the last drinking binge with them, this time the Vodka was colored and I once again had to be escorted back to my quarters by my Russian friends.

I had some real good times in Shangai between the boxing and going on liberty. However, Shanghai wasn't all fun and games. After all, we were there for a reason. And our reason was to guard the American Sector. B Company was frequently assigned guard duty along the Soochow Creek. The Soochow Creek was a very dirty river cluttered with hundreds of sampans, mostly housing very poor Chinese who seemingly lived and died on these sampans with little or no apparent means of support. I would see them leave in the mornings to return in the evenings with wood for cooking and heating.

Like many of the other guard posts throughout Shanghai, those along the Soochow Creek called for strict discipline and alertness, and quite often proved very interesting. One of these posts, manned by two of our Marines, was located on the north side of a bridge spanning the creek; the Japanese guarded the south side of the bridge. Normally this post would be quiet at night because the bridge wasn't used then. Each evening we would lower a heavy wire gate on our end of the bridge and wouldn't open it again until the next morning.

Although night guard duty at the bridge was usually a quite post, it wasn't always a great post. At about 4 a.m. the "honey carts" would begin their daily runs passing within several feet of our bridge guard shack. These carts were simple homemade wagons containing six-foot by two-foot by two-foot box used to haul away the city's prior day's human waste. Each morning the carts, pulled by one man with an end of a rope tied around his waist and the other end tied to the wagon and pushed by a second man, made their rounds, shack by shack, emptying waste buckets into the carts' boxes. The carts' contents were then brought and dumped into the Soochow Creek. There was a continuous flow of these carts from about 4 a.m. until about 9 a.m. The stench was nearly unbearable. When standing this duty, I would light up and smoke cigars in order to help overcome the awful smell. After a night of this my fellow Marines and I were always glad to greet the truck containing our morning relief and take a hot shower as soon as we reached our quarters. Because of these shit carts passing the guard shack, many of the men didn't want to stand the night duty at the Soochow Creek bridge. In addition to not wanting the night duty there, although usually quiet during the night hours, many of the Marines hated the constant turmoil which existed from daylight to dark at the post.

Besides the sampans in the river, the narrow, dirty streets and roads near the Soochow Creek were lined with shacks made of unpainted boards. It seemed as if these shacks had been built by just picking up and fastening together any loose boards that had been found lying around. Throughout the day thousands of Chinese coolies, wearing straw sandals, loose fitting shirts, and baggy pants, pulled around carts loaded with various items to be sold in these shacks. Little kids ran naked through the streets while women, whose feet were bound as children to make their feet pointed, walked about with great difficulty in their similarly pointed shoes. Most of the Chinese constantly seemed to be walking very fast around this area because the Japanese guards wouldn't allow the Chinese to loiter on the Japanese side of the bridge. It was also difficult to recognize between the Japanese, the Chinese, and the Koreans crossing the bridge; they all dressed the same, had similar faces, builds, and characteristics. Nonetheless, with all this constant confusion and turmoil at the bridge, I believe our platoon did a very good job in handling the many difficult situations that arose from time to time.

One of my most memorable situations at the bridge happened at the end of a hot June day. My buddy Bill [William Russell] and I were standing guard duty at the creek, and our friends, the Japanese, were on the other side of the bridge, as usual. Darkness was approaching, and after having a drink of good cold water I told Bill that I was going to light up a cigar and relax while waiting for sundown when we would close the gate for the night. To this Bill had just remarked how nice it was to have some peace and quiet after a hectic day, when all of a sudden we heard the sound of about six rifle shots in rapid succession. Anticipating trouble, we quickly grabbed our rifles and stood at the ready. Suddenly, about 100 Chinese came running across the sixty-foot long bridge. Although I quickly grabbed at the gate and began to lower it, several of the Chinese managed to get by me before I could get it all the way down.

Within seconds two Japanese guards came running across the bridge. As they approached the gate, they pointed their automatic rifles directly at Bill and me and began shouting something in Japanese, which we didn't understand, although I assumed a man they wanted as a result of the shooting had escaped into our sector and they wanted him back. The two Japanese appeared very angry and determined, and for a few moments I had the feeling they were going to fire on us. Telling Bill that we weren't going to raise the gate and let them into our sector, I waved my hands and indicated to the Japanese that they should return to their own side of the bridge. I then told Bill to scowl at them, and with about two feet separating the two Japanese from Bill and myself, the four of us just stood there, exchanging mean stares and pointing our rifles at each other.

I was aware at the time that the Japanese had a rifle company living in a building just across the river, which meant that in the event of serious trouble it was best to not provoke a fight because Bill and I weren't in a very good position with that amount of heavily armed Japanese so close. It was also the last thing the Commandant desired. So, after a few minutes of this standoff, I told Bill to keep looking them straight in the eyes while I called for an interpreter.

It took only about five minutes for an officer to arrive, and after I explained to him the situation he spoke to the Japanese who only then returned to their side of the bridge. Bill and I were very glad that night when our relief truck arrived and we were able to go back to our quarters, take a hot shower, and walk to the mess hall for our fill of hot coffee, eggs, and pancakes.

During the latter months of 1940 and early 1941 we began experiencing trouble with people infiltrating into the American sector and starting riots. It was, incidentally, the Japanese who were creating many of these disturbances, including the starting of strikes and setting of fires. As a result, having to give up our once all-night liberty, we were placed on twenty-four-hour standby. In case of trouble we were ready to board our truck at a moment's notice and could be rolling down the street in a matter of minutes, dressed and equipped for any emergency.

About January 1941 there appeared a noticeable change in the attire of the people entering our sector. Many were now wearing different uniforms and different caps or hats. They all had different cards for identification, and many had long sabers hanging from their waists. I knew the Japanese coming across the bridge were not on goodwill missions, but I also knew there wasn't a hell of a lot we could do. Our objective was to protect American lives and American property, but we didn't have any power to arrest anyone. Nonetheless, I wasn't going to allow the Japanese to harm the Chinese.

In the early spring months of 1941 the fires, rioting, robberies, and murders began occurring more frequently. The daily newspapers were filled with stories of these incidents and I could feel the tension mount among the Chinese. They became worried and nervous because of the fear they had for the Japanese, who would not hesitate or stop at anything at intimidation, even resorting to murder. The Chinese even became afraid of venturing out on their own streets after dark.

On duty along the Soochow Creek during this time I saw thousands of Japanese wearing the differing uniforms and displaying the many different types of ID's crossing one of the three bridges spanning the river and entering the American settlement. With the ongoing violence perpetrated against the Chinese by the Japanese we realized that the Japanese were trying to weaken the solid relationship that existed between the Americans and Chinese, but, without police authority to arrest anyone unless they were creating a disturbance, there was nothing we could do to stop them. And then, when we were called to quell the many disturbances and incidents that were occurring, we were instructed to do so without harming anyone.

In June, at the peak time the Japanese were causing their countless disturbances, rumors began floating around the 4th Marine Regiment that we were going to leave Shanghai to an undisclosed destination. In July I saw my name on the roster of men due to leave the city of Shanghai for training purposes; no destination was listed. This posting caused the creation of hundreds of rumors because no official information had leaked out prior to this bulletin being posted. The rumors mentioned dozens of destinations as to where we were going, with the United States being one of these. Going back to the United States would have been too good to be true. I was hoping to be home in December with the gifts that I had bought for my family because I had previously seen my name listed as one of men due to return to the States in December. But I was soon to find out that this was not to be.

The Chinese were also soon aware of our pending move, and many became worried because it meant they would lose their jobs. They were good workers, always loyal and very dedicated, and I knew they enjoyed working for the Marines and the United States Government. I never saw a Chinese make a bad move. Their motto seemed to be "always please the Marines" because the Marines treated the Chinese with respect, even though most were classed as coolies.

There were also quite a number of our Marines who had Chinese girl friends, and I knew these girls would miss the Marines who provided them with food, whiskey, clothes, and a good place to live. I, myself, didn't live with the Chinese, but my buddies told me that the Chinese were good people and could be trusted. This could not be said, however, for the Russians, who would come over to an apartment with all their friends and drink up all the whiskey in the cupboards.

The Chinese people loved us very much, and on the day of our departure thousands, many with tears running down their cheeks, lined the sidewalks. Countless flags and banners labeled with kind words for the departing 4th Marines were waved at us by the crowds of Chinese as we and our equipment rolled by in the trucks and buses on our way to the Bund where the transport waited.

[Ed left earlier than the majority of the Regiment and may have left on the *Henderson*, the same transport that originally took him to Shanghai. According to one account, an advance party of the 4th Marines was evacuated from Shanghai in October of 1941 on the *Henderson*. The account also states that the Marines' local girlfriends that they had been shaking up with had heard that the Marines were leaving even before the Marines themselves had gotten the word.[6] In addition, in an interview with John Patrick Zimba, John also stated that some of the 4th Marines had been shipped out earlier in 1941 than the bulk of the Regiment. Whether Ed left Shanghai with the advance party in October or he and other 4th Marines left at an even earlier time in 1941, the fact remains that he and several other 4th Marines left Shanghai in 1941, destined for the Philippines, prior to the bulk of the Regiment's departure.]

Shortly after our transport moved up the Yangtze River we were told that our destination was the Philippine Islands. In August 1941 we arrived in the Philippines at Sangley Point. Sangley Point was located across the bay from Manila and several miles from the Cavite Navy Yard. Once there, we set up and lived in tents in an open area adjacent to huge radio towers. A hospital was located not more than a block away from our encampment. For the next several months our company stood guard duty at both the Cavite Navy Yard and a nearby large Navy fuel depot. [It should be noted here that the "bay" that Ed is referring to is not Manila Bay, but a smaller bay, which is part of Manila Bay, just southeast of Manila. Once at Sangley Point and the Cavite Navy Yard, Ed became part of the 700-man 1st Separate Marine Battalion, which was commanded by Lieutenant Colonel John P. Adams.[7]]

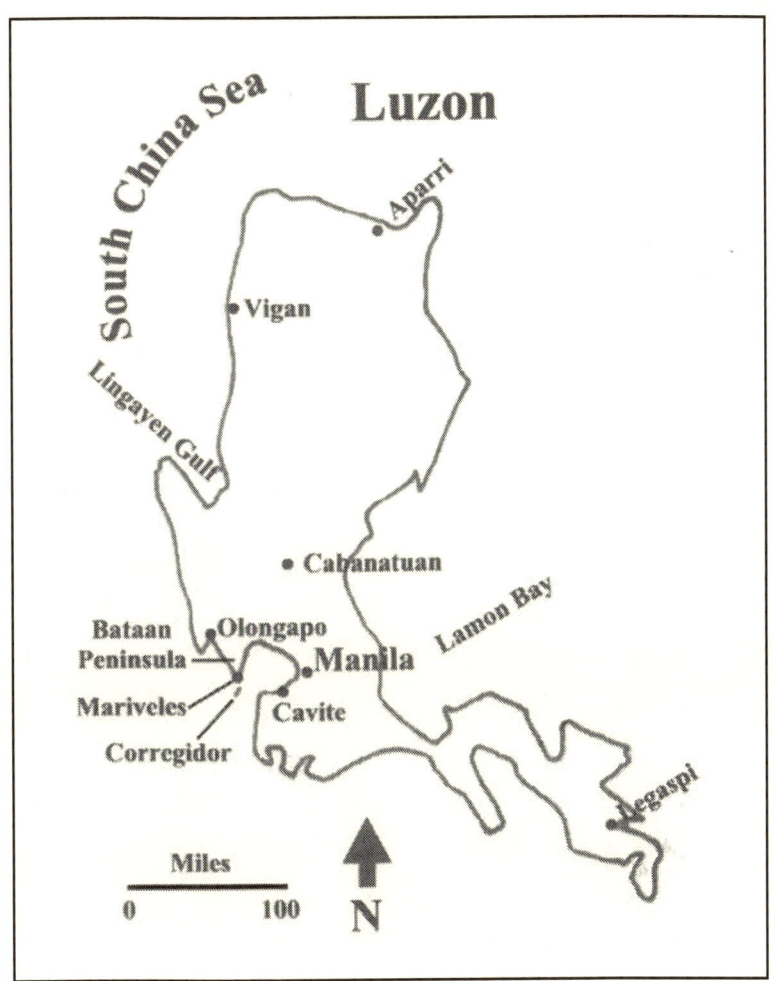

Map 2: Luzon Island

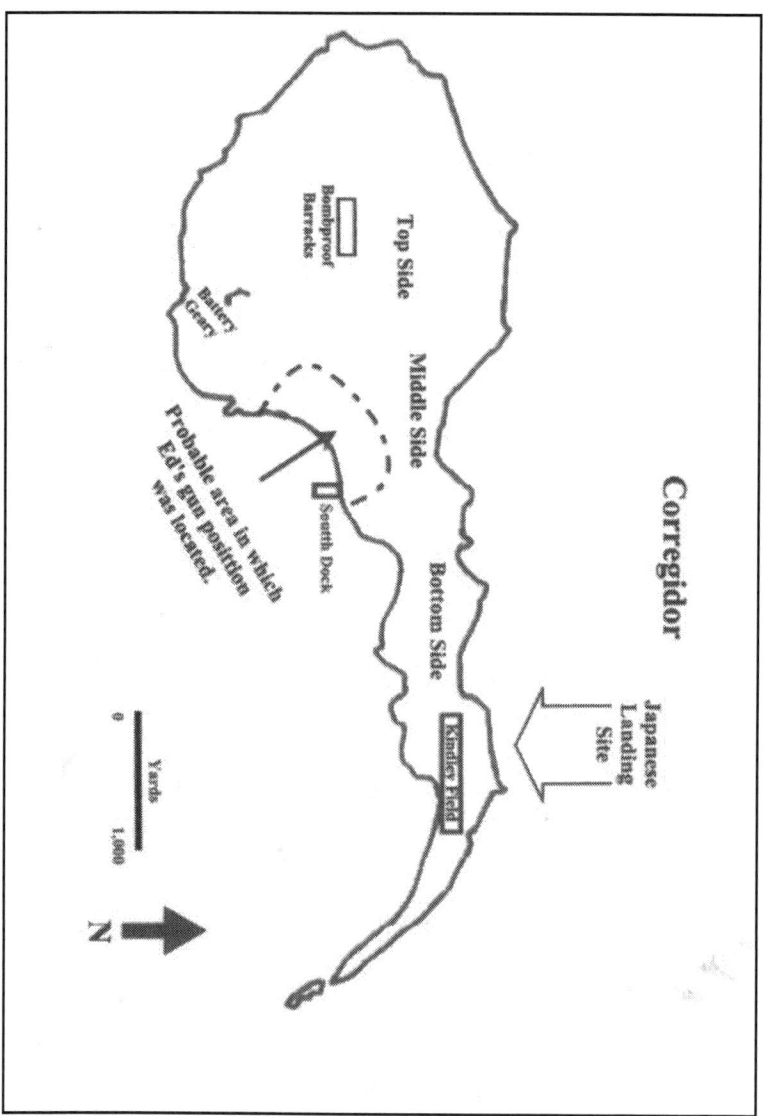

Map 3: Corregidor Island

2 THE WAR BEGINS

On 8 December the air raid sirens began blowing. After several minutes we heard the Japs had bombed Pearl Harbor. Expecting to be hit next the Cavite Navy Yard and all the airfields in the area were immediately put on alert and air raid drills were practiced night and day. [By this time, the rest of the 4th Marine Regiment had also arrived in the Philippines from Shanghai. The bulk of the Regiment evacuated Shanghai for the Philippine Islands on 27 and 28 November 1941 onboard the *SS President Madison* and *SS President Harrison*, respectively, two ex-passenger liners that had been leased for this purpose, landing at Olongapo Navy Yard on 30 November 1941 and 1 December 1941, respectively. Once in the Philippines, the 4th Marine Regiment was initially given the mission of protecting the naval stations on Luzon, mainly at Olongapo and Mariveles.[8]]

We didn't have long to wait. The 10th of December began as a clear and sunny day without even a single cloud in the sky. Being my day off I was spending time in the barracks located next to the Navy Yard when the air raid sirens suddenly began sounding. I quickly dashed outside and gazed up into the sky where I immediately saw an approaching flight of bombers heading directly towards the Navy Yard. I stood there for a while and watched as the bombers drew closer, their sleek, shiny bodies emblazoned with the rising sun symbols on their fuselages stood out clearly against the morning's clear blue sky.

When they were about two miles away I lost no time in finding a low spot in the ground to slide into. Once on the ground I glanced back up at the sky to count the number of bombers; I counted fifty. Within moments, I heard a rattling sound and realized the bombers had released their bombs. Several seconds later I could hear the sound of crashing buildings around me. I lay there in my low spot, covering my head with my hands the best I could. After the sound of the exploding bombs had stopped, I slowly raised my head and looked around. The Navy Yard was scattered with fire, smoke, and debris.

About a minute later I heard the sound of more bombers arriving and again looked up and counted another fifty bombers on the way. Burying my nose once more into the dirt I waited for the release and impact of the bombs. After the new explosions had subsided, I stood up to see additional buildings and boats on fire. I also noticed that the two Marine guards that had been on duty at the main gate of the Navy Yard where now lying motionless near their post. I was about to run and check on them when I heard the sound of more incoming bombers. Counting another fifty approaching, I once again hit my lucky low spot in the ground and for the third time buried my nose in the dirt.

After the release and explosions of this third wave of bombs and again hearing the noise of the surrounding buildings breaking up, I raised my head and glanced around once again, this time noticing that several pieces of shrapnel had hit nearby my little sheltering hole. After waiting for several moments, I stood up hoping the last of the bomber runs had gone by.

[Accounts vary on how many formations and bombers attached. One states that three "V" formations of fifty-four aircraft each attacked Cavite a little past noon on 10 December.[9] Another mentions an eyewitness recalling a formation of fifty-four bombers shortly after 11:30 a.m. on 10 December. The later eyewitness recalled that the formation first made three passes, the first two passes dropping smoke canisters most likely to obtain the windage, dropping their bombs on the third pass. The eyewitness then relates that the bombers made a second bombing run sometime later, although fewer in number.[10] As with all eyewitness accounts, they often vary, especially under extreme and violent circumstances. Either way, as is related by Ed and others, at around noontime on 10 December 1941, the Cavite Navy Yard was attacked by Japanese bombers and sustained massive damage.]

Not hearing any more incoming bombers and deciding that the last of them had probably come and gone, I quickly glanced around at the damaged Navy Yard. Smoke, fire, and debris were everywhere. There were also many dirt and blood covered bodies of my fellow Marines, Navy personnel, and Filipinos lying scattered all over the Navy Yard, many in need of medical attention. Although I couldn't determine the extent of some of the injuries, I could tell that many of these men were barely alive.

Two of my buddies and I, after finding a Navy truck standing idle, quickly began picking up the mangled bodies, placing them into the truck, and taking them to the hospital at Sangley Point.

I drove the truck as the three of us first went to the main gate of the Navy Yard and picked up the two duty Marines who had been standing guard duty there, the two Marines I had just recently seen lying motionless after the second wave of bombs had been dropped. We placed these two and the next three injured men we came across into the truck and took them straight to the hospital. The nurses and doctors were waiting and ready for action upon our arrival. As soon as we pulled up to the ramp the injured were put on carts and wheeled into the hospital. We then quickly headed back to the Navy Yard for more. We made this trip several times, each time bringing five more injured bodies to the hospital. Each time upon our arrival the hospital staff was waiting for our load of wounded. During one of our arrivals at the hospital I noticed that the ramp leading up to the building was splattered with blood, and taking a moment to look around I saw that the entire hospital entrance area was a complete bloody mess.

That evening when darkness came the Navy Yard was still ablaze. A Marine lieutenant instructed us to start digging trenches near the barracks, but soon afterward the company commander arrived and told us to stop. He said we would be moving to the Sangley Point Radio Station for the next several days to await further moves by the Japanese. [It was on this day, 10 December 1941, that the first of several Japanese landings took place on the main Philippine Island of Luzon. This first landing took place on the northern edge of the island.] We then marched back to Sangley Point and to our tents. Once there we were happy to be able to lie down and get some rest after such a very hectic day. It wasn't until we were all assembled a little earlier that evening that we knew exactly how many men had been killed, injured, or listed as missing or unaccounted for during the bombing raid. [Approximately 1,000 civilians were killed, with another 500 wounded during the raid. Five Marines were killed and another eight wounded.[11]] For all of us young Marines, this had been the first taste of war, and I believed we had all matured some.

Two days went by without any further excitement except an occasional sounding of the air raid sirens; two excitement-free days that we all gladly accepted. I imagine that there were planes in the air flying all over the islands during these days, but all we saw or heard of them was the occasional and sporadic air raid siren. [In fact, although 11 December saw the Japanese airfields on Formosan closed by monsoon rains, on 12 and 13 December, the Japanese Air Forces returned, bombing numerous targets throughout the Island of Luzon.[12]]

On the third day, however, the air raid sirens began sounding steadily, and we assumed that there actually were enemy aircraft in the area. In fact, we soon heard word of enemy aircraft in route to the Manila area, which included our location at Sangley Point. We listened intently and several minutes later we could hear the now all too familiar roar of Japanese bombers. Moments later I saw the bombers approaching our area and I realized that the radio towers that overshadowed our tents were probably the bombers' main target. Bombs could easily bring these towers down, crushing any man that happened to be under them. Once this realization hit me, I quickly ran as fast as I could to get away from the area, but by that time the bombers were too close and I couldn't hope to get far enough away. I hit a shallow spot in the ground and quickly buried my face into the turf just as the lead bombers dropped their loads. With a thunderous sound the bombs slammed into the radio towers as well as the ground all around me.

After the bombers had gone, I momentarily waited before raising my head to look at the damage around me. Once I did, I noticed a crater less than a foot away from where I was lying. The tangled steel frameworks of several of the toppled radio towers were also lying near me. Looking around I could see that the entire area was pocked-marked with bomb craters, each six to eight feet deep, including the one next to where I was lying. Every one of our tents was flattened and burning, and the area was scattered with debris. These tents contained all of our gear, which was now destroyed, leaving us with only the clothes on our backs. Our casualties were light, however, only losing one Marine who was hit by shrapnel, and six others requiring first aid. Luckily the hospital nearby, which was still full of casualties from the recent Japanese air raid on the Cavite Navy Yard, was not hit.

[The low-frequency radio towers and the nearby fuel depot were indeed the Japanese targets. The loss of these radio towers meant that U.S. submarines could now only be contacted when on the surface and then only at night.[13] Although Ed states that one Marine was killed and six others were wounded during this air raid, others report that five were killed and eight were wounded. However, this was also relating to the bombing at the nearby fuel depot, also guarded by members of the 1st Separate Marine Battalion.[14] It is also reported that the hospital sustained a direct hit during the initial Cavite air raid on 10 December, and because of this portions of the library in the Marine Barracks were converted to an aid station.[15] This aid station may be what Ed remembers as the hospital.]

At that time I recalled that there were five men housed in the brig attached to the hospital, and I suggested to the lieutenant that we should release these men before another air attack occurred, which the lieutenant then did. After this latest air raid, the officers decided that we might as well leave the area since the Cavite Navy Yard had been destroyed and there was no further need for us in the area. It was pitch-dark that night when we began our march, which would take us to Mariveles. [On 20 December, Colonel Adams received orders to move the 1st Separate Marine Battalion to the Naval Section Base at Mariveles, which was located on the southern most tip of the Bataan Peninsula and about three and a half miles from the Island of Corregidor. The move began on 21 December, with the last of the 1st Separate Marine Battalion evacuating and destroying any military remnants at the Cavite area on Christmas day.[16]]

Many of the local Filipinos from the area that had worked at the Navy Yard, along with others who hated the Japanese, although also hating to leave their homes, accompanied us when we left that night. Many of these refugees packed and brought along what few belongings they had, most even bringing a chicken or two. I noticed that many of these Filipinos were shedding a lot of tears as they departed their homes. A lot of these tears, I believe, were shed due to having had just lost family members killed or injured in the air attacks and not knowing if they, themselves, would ever return to their remaining families and homes.

Orders had been issued for us not to smoke under any circumstances during our march. Although we traveled at night and in areas unfamiliar to us, our officers were very efficient and had a greater knowledge of the country. They also seemed to have had advance information about the movement of the Japanese troops. I believe Filipino scouts may have furnished the officers with these bits of information [Here Ed may be referring to members of the Filipino Scouts Division]. Regardless of where the Japanese troops were, we marched into the jungles of Mariveles [Bataan] and awaited word on any of their movements. Japanese reconnaissance planes flew over the entire area throughout each day giving the Japanese good indications not only on the location of the American troops, but also the types of weapons and equipment we had, and our approximate numbers. [The initial Japanese Air raids on 8 December had destroyed the vast majority of the American Air Forces in the Philippines, leaving the

Japanese in nearly uncontested air superiority over the entire Philippine Islands.]

After several days we heard that Japanese troops had landed on the mainland and were moving in our direction. [Japanese forces landed on Luzon on the 10th, 12th, 21st and 24th of December, with the main landing force coming ashore at Lingayen Gulf on 21 December.] The next morning they began to hit us with their heavy artillery. We started to lose men when their 155s dropped shells in our area. Without Allied air support the Japanese had the ability to shell us with their artillery or bomb us with dive bombers whenever they cared to, and there wasn't anything we could do about it. There wasn't a hell of a lot we could have done if we encountered the Japanese troops either, because all we had were our rifles and .30 and .50 caliber machineguns. We had no alternative but to move back. I remember it was under these circumstances that I spent my Christmas dinner in the jungles of Mariveles [Bataan].

In the meantime, the Japanese were landing more troops every day, and they started moving tanks in our direction. They also bombed the areas to our rear with incendiaries and explosives in attempts to prevent us from conducting a full retreat. We spent the next four days and nights sleepless as we slowly retreated backward to save men for the purpose of defending Corregidor.

The stillness of the nights seemed to create a tension and nervousness that was enhanced whenever the birds and animals made their noises, which tended to keep us awake. The tall jungle trees and dense under growth shielded us from the planes flying overhead, but it also made it easier for the Japanese snipers to get in closer. It boiled down to the fact that neither you nor the enemy wanted to reveal your position. The element of surprise was the key to whether you would kill or be killed. The night was the best time for us to seek out the enemy because we didn't have to contend with the Japanese's advantage of having air cover. [It is possible here that Ed is making a general statement concerning the fighting going on throughout the Island of Luzon. All of the author's research indicates that, with the exception of air attacks, none of the Marines of the 4th Marine Regiment, including the 1st Separate Marine Battalion, came under direct fire from the Japanese until after 29 December, the date they transferred to Corregidor. However, their journey did take them all around Manila Bay and very close to where the Japanese were attempting to cut off all stragglers entering the Bataan Peninsula. Therefore, their march would have taken them close to where the advancing Japanese were.]

It had been agreed that the Marines would be transported to the island of Corregidor to provide a vital part of the island's defense. It was intended that we would establish a beach defense there, and it was to this end that we had been steadily working our way through the Mariveles [Bataan] jungles.

[Since 8 December and notification of the Japanese attack on Pearl Harbor, the 4th Marine Regiment had been busy readying defensive positions around the naval facilities located at Olongapo and Mariveles. The bulk of the 1st Battalion of the 4th Marines (not to be confused with Ed's 1st Separate Marine Battalion) sailed from Olongapo for Mariveles on the morning of 8 December, arriving safely at 11:30 that same day just prior to the initial Japanese air attacks on Luzon. The remaining company of the 1st Battalion, D Company, the heavy weapons company, arrived by truck at Mariveles later that day. On 13 December the 2nd Battalion received the first casualties sustained by the 4th Marine Regiment (the 1st Separate Marine Battalion that Ed was a member of was not yet officially a part of the 4th Marine Regiment) when bomb fragments during an air raid at Olongapo hit Private First Class Neil P. Iovino.[17]

The joint defense plan for the Philippines called for the transfer of the Marines to Army operational control. Admiral Thomas Hart, USN, Commander-in-Chief, Asiatic Fleet, and Marine Lieutenant Colonel William T. Clement, Fleet Marine Officer, had argued against such a move from the time the Japanese attacked Pearl Harbor. However, they were finally overruled, and General Richard K. Sutherland, USA, MacArthur's chief of staff, ordered Colonel Howard to proceed with the 4th Marines to Corregidor as soon as possible to take over the beach defenses.[18]]

The last night in these jungles found us waiting for pitch darkness for our march to the beach to board the several barges that would take us across the bay to Corregidor, a trip that ultimately went smoothly. Almost everyone agreed that one day the Japanese would climb the many rocks and crevices of the Corregidor cliffs, and I believe that the Army was happy to see us Marines arrive to help augment their forces on the "Rock," as the island of Corregidor was called. [The 1st Separate Marine Battalion crossed the channel to Corregidor on 26 December. The 2nd Battalion, along with the forward echelon of the Headquarters and Service Companies, made the trip on 27 December, with the remainder of the regiment, including the 1st Battalion, making the trip on 29 December.[19]]

At about 9 A.M. on the morning of 29 December, just as the Marine units were being organized at our new home on Corregidor, the air raid sirens began to sound. In a matter of a few minutes a flight of Japanese bombers were overhead and dropping their load of bombs directly on the main barracks Topside. Everyone, however, was able to safely find cover and no casualties were suffered. This was the first air raid we experienced on the Rock, and I thought it to be a warning of what could be expected in what turned out to be our next five months. [This was indeed the first Japanese air raid of the war on Corregidor, and for that matter, the first attack, whether from aircraft, cannon, or infantry that Corregidor would suffer in the next four plus months. Although Ed was unaware of any casualties, Corporal Verle W. Murphy was killed and nine other Marines were wounded in the attack. The total casualties on Corregidor during this initial attack were twenty killed and eighty wounded.[20]] Throughout our stay on Corregidor I was often to hear the Army remark that Corregidor was the Rock that could not be penetrated or fall, but I believe in reality we all found it possible for any fortress to fall.

[Corregidor, also known as Fort Mills, was affectionately known as the "Rock" by many of those who served on her. A little over a mile wide at its widest, it was three and a quarter miles long. The island was divided into three sections; "Bottomside," "Middleside," and "Topside." One of the most impressive structures of the island was the system of tunnels. These tunnels, begun being constructed in the early 1930's, housed, among other things, a 300-bed hospital, a naval communications center, fuel and ammunition storage, and housing for General MacArthur, Philippine President Manuel Luis Quezon Antonia y Molino (commonly referred to simply as Quezon or President Quezon), U.S. Commissioner Francis Bowes Sayre, and their staffs and families. Fort Mills and her sister island forts, Hughes, Frank and Drum, were designed to guard the Manila Bay from any threat from the sea.[21]]

Almost immediately after the air raid, squads were organized amongst the Marines, barbed wire entanglements were setup along the beach, and the men began building gun positions at strategic locations in which were mounted .30 and .50 caliber machineguns. Besides these machineguns, we were also armed with our good old-faithful 1903 [Springfield] rifles, a .45 Colt, and a supply of grenades.

A lieutenant had picked the place for my gun position, giving me no choice but to put it where he suggested. Being at the edge of the top of a cliff overlooking the bay, it was in the open and fully exposed. And being made of wooden planks, rocks, and dirt, it could also be easily penetrated by a shell or shrapnel, affording practically no protection during any shelling or bombing. After watching several men in the following days cut down during artillery barrages and bombings as they tried to run for cover, I decided this was a tactic that wasn't for me. So I looked nearby for better shelter.

With a little searching I was able to discover an old Army pillbox about thirty feet below my position. It was old and had apparently been around for a long time, but was still in good shape, and only a direct bomb hit would likely cause any injury to someone safely inside it. I knew that during a bombing raid or shelling, when the shrapnel was ricocheting all over my gun position, I wouldn't have to worry if I were in this pillbox, so that's where I went whenever I was manning my post and the bombings and shellings started.

Every night I stayed at my gun position because it was at night that I expected the Japanese to attack. I had a hell of a time getting any of the other men to pull duty with me at my position during these nights. I had the same problem during the daytime whenever we were receiving any of our many shellings.

Every day we could either expect a flight of enemy bombers or the Japanese to shell the hell out of us with their 155s. One day alone it seemed as though the air raid sirens had sounded continuously all day long, and I counted fifteen separate air-attacks. The Japanese also used 240-millimeter siege guns against us, which would create extensive damage wherever their shells hit. Many of these bombings and shellings scored direct hits on the Army's big 12- and 14-inch seacoast guns, damaging their mechanisms and putting them out of action until they could be repaired. [Corregidor had two batteries each of 12-inch rifled guns and 12-inch mortars. Fort Drum, a nearby smaller fortified island, had a battery of 14-inch rifled guns positioned in a metal turret.] Gradually the heavy shellings and bombings completely knocked these big guns out.

Direct hits on the guns would send shrapnel flying in every direction, many times killing or injuring as many as five or six men at a time. I believe men were killed or injured, and guns, especially the big 12- and 14-inch ones, were knocked out or rendered useless during every attack, either by the shellings or the bombings. My lieutenant told me that one busy day as many as 16,000 shells hit Corregidor, probably killing and seriously injuring hundreds. [It was estimated that on 4 May 1942 16,000 Japanese shells hit Corregidor.] It wasn't long before the Japanese realized that our guns could not reach their aircraft, allowing the Japanese to stage their air raids without interruption. About all the Marines could do was to improve their gun positions with more camouflage and dig trenches in the area with the hope that if necessary the machineguns may still be useful one day.

During the days that I wasn't working at my assigned gun position, I would help the Army fire their 12-inch gun positioned not far from my machinegun nest. [The battery that Ed is referring to is most probably Battery Geary, one of the two 12-inch mortar batteries located on Corregidor. The two 12-inch rifles batteries could only traverse out to sea and the other 12-inch mortar battery, Battery Way, was inactive until just prior to the Japanese invasion of Corregidor due to lack of qualified gunners.] Quite a number of Army men had been killed or injured, and due to the day after day shelling some had become nervous or fearful. Being asked to help I was happy to do so and was always ready at any time because it gave me an opportunity to get back at the enemy who had killed so many of our men at Pearl Harbor. I derived a lot of satisfaction at knowing that I was killing Japs. I also enjoyed working with the Army gunners.

My job at the 12-inch gun itself was easy. All I had to do was help carry the powder to the gun prior to it being readied to fire. The Army's big gun positions were constructed of concrete with the gun centered inside a circular forty-foot diameter pit. Located in one corner was the powder room with its steel door. We would dash back into this powder room and shut the steel door as soon as we delivered the powder to the gun.

Many times we had small private wars going on between our 12-inch gun and the Japs with their 155s and 240-millimeter siege guns. Moments after we fired a round towards Bataan and were safely tucked away inside the powder room we would hear the roar of the incoming shell fired by the Japs in response. About two seconds later we would hear the shell land and explode inside the pit, its fragments ricocheting off the gun and appearing to hit everywhere inside the pit, including the powder room's steel door. Standing inside this powder room during these shellings, I realized how fortunate I was to have a safe place to avoid being hit with shrapnel.

Time after time the Japs made direct hits on the gun itself. They evidently had perfectly zeroed in on us, which told me that the Japanese had been obtaining information for years on the position of the army and navy installations. This made me believe that the Japanese were not the most stupid people in Asia as I once thought, because they accomplished a lot before the war. [Although Japanese spies had gathered much information prior to the war, with the surrender of Bataan, the Japanese captured maps of Corregidor and its major gun positions.]

1220 Days

One sunny afternoon I was loafing in my gun position when I heard the Japs start their shelling. But this time I noticed the shells were falling in the bay. I then saw a small Navy craft enter the bay area between Corregidor and Fort Hughes. The Japanese had seen this boat and were trying to hit it with their shells, which were exploding all around the little craft as it zigzagged through the bay attempting to avoid being hit. The small boat seemed to be making for a dock, which stuck out about thirty feet into the bay just below the cliff from my gun position. I continued to watch as the boat finally managed to get out of the Japs' sight and tie up at the dock. Once tied up, the Navy crew hurriedly ran for cover.

I figured that the Navy crew had some food supplies aboard and I inquired of them as to whether they did. They replied, "Sure, if you want to risk going out to the boat yourself." By that time the shells had stopped landing in the area, so I walked up the dock and climbed onboard the boat, where I immediately noticed cans of peaches and pears. We had not had any fruit in the chow line for some time, so I grabbed several cans of the peaches and returned to my gun position.

I didn't think the Navy crew would stay around any great length of time because they were of no use if they stayed there in the harbor, and no doubt they were scheduled to move on to another destination. A half hour later they indeed started their engines and were off, this time in the opposite direction they had come from and one that appeared that the Japs did not have a battery facing.

By 5 May 1942 thousands [Ed may mean thousands throughout the Philippine Islands] of Army, Navy, and Marine personnel had been killed or injured by the continuous shellings and bombings. The big 12- and 14-inch seacoast guns had all been knocked out of action and many of the mounted .30 and .50 caliber machineguns had likewise been destroyed. Bombs had wrecked the majority of the buildings and all the trees were either knocked down or cut in half. The Japanese were aware of the fact that our defense had been lessened to such an extent that they were quite positive they could stage an assault without effective resistance.

Early that evening [5 May] the Japs started shelling the Rock, releasing a monstrous attack with their 155s and 240-millimeter siege guns. The shelling continued without letup, and we were losing men. After it became pitch dark, the skies became filled with thousands of Japanese flares. It looked like hundreds of 4th of July fireworks all being displayed at one same time and was actually a beautiful sight with the flares lighting up the sky for what seemed like miles. However, in actuality, it was not a beautiful sight for us Americans to behold. These flares were being launched for a purpose.

While the flares were lighting up the sky several hundred barges loaded with thousands of Japanese troops were landing below the overhanging cliffs of Corregidor. As soon as these barges came into view the Marines strafed them with machinegun fire. Thousands of the Japanese troops were killed outright while still onboard the barges by this machinegun fire. Hundreds of others staggered off the barges and fell before reaching the shore. Observers noted that many of the barges were covered with dead Japanese bodies and that the water was filled with the bodies of dead or bleeding and screaming wounded Japanese soldiers. [Of the 2,400 Japanese troops in the first wave, less than 800 made it to shore and 60 percent of the landing craft and supporting gunboats were destroyed.]

Even with those killed on the beaches, hundreds of Japanese were attempting to climb the steep cliffs' craggy edges. The expert rifle fire coming from the Marine rifles hit many of the Japanese as soon as they reached the top, but, like the machinegun fire just before, this also did not stop the Japanese advance. It appeared as though the Japs were attempting the same method of suicidal tactics they would later employ in many of the Pacific islands, where it was do or die as they pressed forward with no special defensive maneuver. Due to the previous American losses on the Rock, I would have to say that we were outnumbered at a ratio of close to twenty to one, and there were just too many of the Japs to stop. Despite all of their losses, several thousand of the Jap troops made it over the top and with their automatic weapons managed to kill a large number of Army and Marine troops.

The Americans fought hard, with many individual hand to hand fights taking place. No one writes about those brave men who fought because they were expected to do so and died only because they were outnumbered. The real heroes are the men who died on the battlefield of Corregidor. [Although Ed's description of the fighting on Corregidor is quite accurate, his battalion, re-designated as 3rd Battalion, 4th Marine Regiment upon their transfer to Corregidor, was assigned an area located in the "Middleside" section of the Island, well away from the locations of the actual fighting. The bulk of the fighting itself took place on "Bottomside."]

By daylight fighting had ceased in the majority of the vital areas, although there were occasional bursts of fire from many of the outlying positions. I believe most of the men had arrived at the conclusion that to continue was hopeless, and resistance had dwindled after the sleepless night. About 9 a.m. I began to notice that white flags in the form of towels or any piece of available cloth appeared throughout the island, indicating that we had surrendered.

For a time all was quiet, and it seemed to me as though the fighting had stopped. Although I had received no official word, a buddy told me that General Wainwright had surrendered to the Japanese. [At 12:00 noon on 6 May 1942 General Jonathan Wainwright, who had assumed command upon MacArthur's departure from the Philippines, was forced to surrender all Allied forces throughout the Philippine Islands. Colonel Howard, upon hearing that he was forced to surrender was reported to have put his face in his hands and murmured that he was the first Marine officer to ever surrender a regiment.[22]] It was quiet for about thirty minutes when suddenly I heard the noise of Japanese planes approaching my area. I then saw three dive-bombers swoop down and fire at several of the gun positions in my area, including mine. The dive-bombers made at least half a dozen dives on these gun positions with bullets hitting mine by the hundreds, or at least so it seemed. Every time the dive-bombers strafed me I continued to fire a steady stream of lead up at them hoping that I might score a hit.

On one of these passes the dive-bombers scored a direct hit on a building near my position. Chunks of concrete flew in all directions, sending one crashing on top of my gun position filling it with smoke and dust and hitting the top of my machinegun. By the time this dust had settled, the planes had gone. My machinegun had been damaged beyond repair and the rocks and lumber that had been part of the protection of the top of my hole had all fallen inside and I was barely able to crawl out of my gun pit. All the nearby buildings had been destroyed and were burning, and the entire area was covered with debris.

For a brief time it was quiet, then suddenly I heard the noise of three motor-launches approaching the dock below what was left of my position. I at once noticed the motor-launches were flying the Japanese Rising Sun flag. It made me mad to think that those dirty bastards had strafed the hell out of me just thirty minutes before the launches pulled up.

I quickly tossed my grenades, rifle, Colt .45, and wrecked machinegun into the bay. I thought many times since my return that I should probably have tossed the grenades at the launches, maybe killing a dozen Japs and temporarily halting their moves. After all, they had just killed a few more Army soldiers and Marines in those last dive-bombings they made on us. But I realize that if I had thrown the grenades the Japs would have killed me and then shot friends of mine who were already beginning to assemble with the other men that were coming forward from the different areas of the island.

If I had not been so close to the dock I may have thought about waiting to see what was going to happen before going there myself. As it was I can safely say that I felt very small and lowered my head as I walked towards the group of my fellow Americans beginning to assemble at the foot of the dock. Unless it happens to you, one is unable to understand exactly how it feels to walk towards the enemy with your hands raised above your head. I can just imagine how terrible General Wainwright felt when he was forced to surrender all the Philippine Islands and thousands of troops to the Japanese knowing that all the troops would become prisoners of war.

I couldn't help but notice the expression of joy and triumph on the faces of the Japanese as they all stood up in their launches to see us Americans gathering at the head of the dock. Just as soon as they had tied their launches up to the dock, the Japs jumped out of their boats and with fixed bayonets came running towards us yelling commands of *"Koodo, koodo, speedo, speedo, kiotski."* We soon came to understand this to mean "Attention, attention, hurry up and stand at attention in ranks for inspection."

Everybody stood with their hands over their head until one of the Japs came by and searched them. When I lowered my hands too early, a little Jap ran up, hollered, *"Kiotski,"* and put his bayonet against my stomach forcing me to raise my hands back over my head. Our watches were the first things taken when they searched us; they then took any rings we had on. A laugh or movement by an American while being searched was rewarded with a hit from a Japanese rifle butt. After the searches were completed, the Japanese marched us to an open area along the beach, which would prove to be our little haven for the next five or six days.

[Among the roughly 13,700 American and Filipinos that surrendered on Corregidor, 1,487 were 4th Marines; 167 of these Marines were wounded, 89 others had been killed in battle or died of wounds.[23]]

3 INTO CAPTIVITY – CABANATUAN - PHILIPPINES

We spread our blankets on the sand and rubble of the beach and sat down. It was not long before we discovered that this was not to be a place of rest but a stopover while we worked carrying bags of sugar, rice, flour, and other foodstuff to a Japanese transport waiting a short distance off shore. With their constant commands of *"Hiako, hiako,"* meaning faster, faster and *"Shigoto tocson,"* work very much, the Japanese had a steady stream of men carrying supplies out of the tunnel [the large Malinta Tunnel]. We worked from daylight to dark while being continually prodded by the Japs and their bayonets. They didn't work us at night, however, probably not wanting any of us to escape in the darkness.

The nights were mighty chilly, and the thousand or so of us there on the beach had to huddle together to share space and blankets. To my surprise, though, the Japs allowed us to build fires, which helped. The waters of Manila Bay served as our washing and bathing supply, but not wanting us to escape, the Japanese roped off the beach to keep us from wandering too far away. On the second night of our stay on the beach it rained, and before the night was over everyone was soaked and shivering; we were all glad to see the sun shining the next morning.

We were not given anything to eat during this period. I imagine the Japs thought that if we couldn't steal enough to eat while we were going in and out of the tunnel carrying the food to the transport, then we could just starve. It was basically every man for himself; although, if a buddy didn't get anything because he was afraid of getting caught and punished by getting the hell beat out him, we usually insured that he had some food. Every trip I made into the tunnel I would try to come out with some food. I looked for sugar, raisins, chocolate, or cookies; anything that wasn't too bulky and easily noticeable by the guards. I did, however, manage to sneak out a can of fruit every day and at night divided it with a few of the other men.

In a situation like we were in we had to remain cool. Getting excited or angry and striking our captors would usually result in the prisoner being bayoneted or shot. I was tempted hundreds of times to slug those little men, but the odds were always stacked against me and I would remember the old saying that everything was fair in love and war.

We must have moved several tons of food from the tunnel to the transport; food which I believed the Japanese used to furnish their troops on the many islands they held at the time. During the fighting on Corregidor I was never inside the tunnel itself and now I could hardly believe there were so much supplies stored there. We worked in and out of it for five days.

I remember that the sixth day on the beach was a bright and sunny day. It was that day that our guards began pushing and prodding us down the beach and hollering, "*Koodo, koodo, speedo, speedo.*" Glancing in the direction in which we were being herded, I noticed that about a dozen barges had been anchored a short distance from the shore about fifty yards down the beach. We were being moved from Corregidor. A group of disabled men were left behind, and I heard later that they had been left to clean up the mess on the Rock and to bury the dead.

Within a short time after we left the shores of Corregidor in the barges I could see the city of Manila in the distance, and in another fifteen minutes I noticed we were headed towards Dewey Boulevard. It was then that I glanced back and took my last look at Corregidor. I have never been back to the Rock since. I have never cared to go back and see all the ruins and the site of our surrender—too many memories would surface in doing so.

Just as soon as the barges were within fifty feet of the Manila shoreline the Jap guards began hollering, "*Koodo, koodo,*" telling us to hurry up and get off the barges. In many of the spots the water was a dozen feet deep and many of the injured men had to be helped ashore. Everyone was soaked by the time we finally got there. The first thing I noticed once we finally struggled ashore was the thousands of Filipinos lined up along the boulevard. There was no doubt that the Japs had planned this as a demonstration to downgrade us prisoners and impress upon the Filipinos that Japan was more powerful than the United States and that the Japanese would help the Filipinos.

I remember that the time of day was about 11 a.m. It was hot as hell and we were all soaking wet from having to swim and wade ashore from the barges. It was in this condition that the Japanese forced us to march though the streets of Manila. After several hours of marching at a good pace in the hot Philippine sun without any stops for water or rest, many of the men were getting thirsty and weak. Three-fourths of us were only wearing shorts and shoes. Perspiration ran down our faces and into our eyes, and our backs glistened in the bright sunshine. It did no good to ask for water because the men who asked were greeted with a sneer and a loud shout of *"Mizu ni"* from the Japanese guards, which meant no water. Each time an American fell to the street, the Japanese guards would yell their familiar *koodo, koodo,* this time meaning get up, get up. If the American didn't rise immediately he was repeatedly clubbed with the butt of a rifle, or worse. Several times during the march I heard the crack of rifle fire and knew that another American had been shot and lie dead in the street. I hoped some Filipino would pick up the body and bury it in a marked grave.

I believe that many of the Filipino civilians had been forced out of their homes to witness this parade of captured Americans marching through Manila. Some of the Filipino civilians jeered us, but more cheered and at times even tried to help us, even though every time one of them tried to give us water they were hit with a rifle butt. Many of the Filipinos also gave us the "V" sign for victory when the Japs weren't looking.

[The Japanese indeed intended this march as a demonstration and had forcibly herded the Filipino civilians into the streets to witness the great Japanese triumph over the western powers; but it backfired. The Japanese had just invaded the Philippine Islands, inflicting thousands of casualties among both the Filipino military and civilian populations. As a result, the Filipino people despised the Japanese as much, if not more, than the Americans did. Many of these civilians along the march willingly incurred great risks to their own lives in trying to give aid to both the American and Filipino captives (members of the Philippine Scouts Division that had fought on and were captured when Corregidor surrendered were also among this group being paraded) in the way of water and food. Although it proved hard and nearly always deadly for an American to successfully dart into the throngs of Filipino civilians crowded along the streets and alleyways, some of the Filipino soldiers were able to do just that, quickly mingling with the friendly crowd and securing their freedom.]

About four hours into our march, being tired, I fell a few times. But each time thinking, "I will not let you little yellow bastards get me down," I was on my feet before a guard had a chance to strike me with his rifle. Quite a number of men fainted due to the heat, and if a Filipino civilian were near they would douse the man with water. If the man recovered quickly the guard might allow him to continue the march. If the man didn't recover fast enough, he was either bayoneted or shot. The choice of this action or non-action towards the prisoner solely depended upon the guard at hand. Many of the guards were sadistic and enjoyed watching an American beg to live, while others would not kill as quickly. I saw plenty of American blood flow that day from bayonets and rifle butts.

I noticed that if someone complained and displayed resentment the Japanese guards would hit and hurt that person more. When we started walking slower, because our legs became weary and heat exhaustion made us weak, we were greeted with the familiar *koodo, koodo* and a rifle butt or their favorite tool, a whip, would help speed us up. When noticing others getting weak, I tried giving them encouragement by saying, "Come on partner, don't give up. Let's show them we can take anything they dish out." I noticed that the guards liked to work on me because, at six feet, I was so tall. It seemed to make them feel good to continually walk alongside me and continue bantering me with a mess of Japanese I didn't understand. Several guards, however, understood English, and if you called them a son-of-a-bitch, you had it. The punishment for this infraction called for death by rifle fire.

After four or five hours of this continuous marching in the hot sun our mouths were parched, our lips were burnt, our backs were red and burnt, our legs ached, and our feet were tired, but what I regret the most was the fact that the dirty Japs laughed and joked about our predicament. Deep inside of me I had the feeling that at some time at a later date our turn would come. I knew that some Marines in the South Pacific would kill the enemy for me and the others, but I regret to say that I never did get the opportunity to strike back myself.

After six hours of this continuous marching through all the main streets and many of the side streets of Manila, the sun was beginning to sink below the horizon and I realized the march would soon end because I was sure the Japs wouldn't march us after dark. The Japanese knew, as well as we did, that the possibility of making contact with friendly Filipinos was better after dark, and the opportunity to escape would have been too great in the darkness. At about that time I could see the walls of Bilibid Prison several blocks away. The lights mounted on the prison walls were bright, lighting up the surrounding area. [Bilibid Prison was a POW camp located in Manila. It was originally built as a civilian prison and used as such prior to the war. Throughout the war, however, it was used by the Japanese as a sort of transit camp for POWs coming and going through the Manila docks. In addition, according to a 1945 report by the United States Office of the Provost Marshal General, the Japanese used it as a POW hospital, although very little medicines were supplied to the American military doctors who ran the hospital.[24]]

It was apparent that the Japanese expected the possibility of an uprising at the prison when we, a tired, unshaven, hungry, thirsty, and haggard group of prisoners, marched through its heavy iron grilled gates that evening. Besides the guard shack being manned with ten guards armed with a machinegun and bayonet-fixed rifles, the Japanese also had about one hundred extra guards spread around the inside and outside of the prison walls. Just in case we had thoughts of going over the prison's twenty-foot high wall, there were three 3-inch diameter wires on top of the wall, and we were informed that they were hot [electrified]. However, none of this mattered that night; we were too tired to cause any trouble.

What I really wanted was about a half-gallon of water, which I did finally get after the Japs were satisfied everyone was accounted for. I was surprised that they cooked up a big pot of rice, which they called *lugao*. *Lugao* was almost like water in that you could drink it. They also cooked a barrel of tea, which I didn't like. Although the prison had the usual cellblocks with very small, approximately one-foot square, windows, the Japanese didn't care if we fell asleep on the grass. Being tired, after eating the *lugao* and drinking the water, I laid down on the grass on my blanket. Within five minutes I was out for the night.

About 5:30 a.m. I heard a guard hollering, "*Bango, bango, speedo, speedo,*" which we all took for hurry up and get up. Although guards then went throughout the POWs occasionally poking one of us with their rifles to make sure everyone was getting up for the count (called *bango* by the Japanese), I believe everyone had already learned their lessons the previous day and most moved before a guard had the opportunity to use his rifle. The Japanese had again prepared *lugao* for our breakfast, which became the usual fare for our meals. [*Lugao* became the staple of the Japanese held POWs during the war. As Ed relates, it consisted of very watery rice; so watery it was usually nearly drinkable.] And again they served us a cup of tea. The Japs told us that we wouldn't be getting anymore rice or tea until we reached our destination that night, and, although I didn't know it at the time, I could have used a little more chow that morning, because between our breakfast and dinner was roughly twenty-five kilometers of marching and a hot, crowded, and stuffy train ride.

After we finished our breakfast we were marched to the Manila railroad yard where three cattle cars awaited us. Once there, the guards yelled their usual *speedo, speedo* and indicated for us to hurry and get into the cattle cars. They pushed and shoved us in, finally even using their rifle butts to hurry us up. About 2,000 of us were all jammed into the three cattle cars. It really was crowded as hell, so crowded that we had to stand up until we reached the end of the line. It reminded me of the times back in Wisconsin when the cattle were shipped by rail. It was also a hot day. Between this heat and the overcrowding, numerous arguments broke out among the men along the way, although there was no real space in the cars for any actual fighting to break out.

Our train stopped at a small town called Panginay. As soon as the guards opened the cattle car doors they began yelling their *speedo, speedo* to hurry us off the train. We all had to jump down off the cars, and in a hurry. Quite a number of the men were disabled and couldn't jump down. The guards just jumped in and pushed these injured men out. I didn't like that at all and was ready to start slugging a guard when a buddy said to me, "Take it easy, Ed. You can't win." Although I knew he was right, I still didn't like the guards treating our men like that.

After the railroad cars were empty, the guards lined us up four abreast, with the line extended for about a mile. A short Japanese lieutenant was in charge of the march; he had a long saber hanging at his side. After it appeared as though there was some semblance of a line, he pulled his saber from its scabbard, lifted it high in the air, and, wanting everyone to hear him, gave the command in a very loud voice, "*Kiotskiiii*," drawing out the *iii*. Damn near everyone heard him too. We began our forty-kilometer march to our destination, Cabanatuan.

As we marched down the gravel country road towards Cabanatuan our Japanese guards, who were stationed with their bayonet-fixed rifles at the ready alongside us at about thirty-foot intervals, kept us at a steady pace. I noticed many of these guards tried to look real tough in an attempt to impress us. The scowls on their faces were probably to discourage any escape attempt. By this time, after all of the marching we had done as

Japanese prisoners, I could almost read their minds, and by the expression on their faces I could tell whether they were angry. I could tell a mean, surly guard from one that would strike you only if necessary.

By mid-day it had become very hot, and having already marched about fifteen kilometers we all began to show the effects. Our faces were flushed and red and our bare backs were burnt. When a number of the men asked the guards for water, the guards just laughed and muttered to each other in Japanese and shouted the same reply as during our march in Manila, "*Mizu Ni!*" A few of the weaker men began to fall to the gravel road. As each one fell, a guard would rush over with his rifle butt at the ready and kick and jab the prisoner with his boot and rifle butt.

Blisters began forming on the bottom of our feet. As a result, quite a number of men took off their shoes and tossed them into the roadside ditches. They were destined to wish they had kept their shoes later on if they ended up going on any of the work details. Towards the end of the day a large number of men had to be helped along, either by words of encouragement or just by grasping a hand and supporting the man for awhile, enabling him to finish the several kilometers left before we stopped for the night. At about 6 p.m., as darkness was approaching, we were halted for the night. Believe me, everyone was happy for the stop; our bodies were really tired, and they were also burnt from the sun. I recall my nose was red as hell and was already beginning to peel.

Barely had we stopped our march and sat down that evening when it began to rain—I realized it would be a very long and hard night. The night did have one bright spot, however. The Japs cooked some *lugao* and tea, and it felt very good to get something hot on such a wet night.

After the Japs found *bango* to be right, we spread our blankets on the grass in the ditch and tried to get some much-needed rest. But this soon became difficult. The rain became more intense and, becoming very cold, I shivered most of the night and didn't sleep more than two hours. And even these few hours of sleep proved to be quite un-restful, being filled with dreams of beatings.

As the next morning approached I heard the Japanese guards yelling their *bango, bango*. Waking up, I realized that I had been lying in a puddle of water. After we were counted, the guards served us our *lugao* and tea and were then soon calling out, "*Speedo, speedo,*" and, "*Kiotski,*" for us to line up in neat columns of four for our continued march. Five minutes later we were again marching down the road. The hot sun that day, for a change, felt good, soon taking away the chill. It's my belief the guards were anxious to get to Cabanatuan because they kept yelling *speedo, speedo* throughout the march. I too was anxious to get to our destination—this was our third day of marching and we were all getting very tired.

On this final day of the march one could really tell the men from the boys. After three hours of marching our bodies again were burnt to a state of irritation. We were all so red that we looked like Indians. We had no hats and many of us became dizzy in the hot sun. I saw several of the men fall from heat exhaustion only to be hit with rifle butts. It became tougher to go on with each additional hundred yards to the point that just putting one foot ahead of the other was a challenge in itself, and again we weren't given any water. My lips became parched and my mouth so dry I didn't even have enough saliva left to spit. I was really looking forward to a cold drink of water at the end of our march.

A buddy of mine from Shanghai, who was a sergeant, had managed to bring along a sea bag full of cloths all the way from Corregidor. With only about five kilometers left to go to Cabanatuan he couldn't carry it any further, so he tossed it into the roadside ditch. Wanting to prove that a sergeant could not do a job as well as a private, a private first class, or a corporal under such adverse conditions in wartime as we were now experiencing, I picked up the bag and carried it.

An individual's performance during peacetime cannot reveal how that person will react when the enemy is in control. Being forced to march until we dropped, beaten with clubs, fists, rifles, or a sheathed bayonet while all the time being provided with only a starvation diet caused loss of weight and strength, all of which made us want to strike back. It was only our better judgment telling us to have patience that kept us from doing so.

In spite of their treatment of us on this march, I don't think the Japs really wanted to lose too many of us because they wanted to be able to ship as many prisoners as possible to the different work details at the nearby airfields and the docks at Manila. Nonetheless, I estimated that there were only about 1,200 of us Americans left when we finally marched through the gates of Cabanatuan.

Somehow, during all the confusion of entering the compound and assembling for a *bango*, four men had turned around and walked outside the fence. Several minutes later the Jap guards noticed the four men walking down the road. Immediately, fixing their bayonets, several of the guards ran after the four POWs. When the guards caught up with the escapees, the guards repeatedly hit the four escapees and then returned them to the compound. When these four prisoners were back inside the compound, Lieutenant Shimoko, the camp commander, loudly called out the command *kiotski* and uttered a few more vengeful words towards the four escapees. Then, under orders from Lieutenant Shimoko, several Japanese guards blindfolded the four attempted escapees and shot them in full view of the rest of us prisoners as a warning for us not to try to escape.

The camp itself, at Cabanatuan, consisted of about a dozen newly built bamboo shacks, each about eighty feet long and twenty feet wide. There were no trees and very little grass in the compound. The whole camp area was covered with a soft clay soil, and it would rain every afternoon, which left the compound a muddy mess. We were warned that shoes were not allowed to be worn in the shacks because of the rains and the muddy mess they caused. This was a rule that was strictly enforced by the guards.

It was hot in the camp whether one just loafed around the camp or worked on one of the two work details. These work details consisted of a burial detail and a detail cutting and carrying wood to the camp for fuel to cook the rice and onion soup, which was our regular diet for the three months that I was there. I didn't care at all for the burial detail because of the smell, nor did I like to see the emaciated bodies. For a short time the burial ground was inside the camp, but the daily death count soon increased by the hundreds when dysentery hit the compound. The bodies were then carried outside the camp and dumped en masse into a large shallow grave or hole. [At Cabanatuan the death rate was 100 per day. Within six months 5,000 Americans died as Japanese captives.[25]]

Those dirty little yellow men withheld food from us and enjoyed watching us gripe about being allowed only one canteen cup full of water per man each day. The camp had several water faucets that the guards would turn on periodically. There would always be a long line of prisoners waiting at these faucets just to get their one cupful. Several of the guards were especially rough. When one of these guards was on duty he would enjoy shutting off the water faucet before all the men could get a cupful of water, all the while wearing a smirk on his face. Many were the times this happened, leaving twenty or so men waiting in line for their water. I was damn mad when I was one of those who was caught short and missed getting my only cup of water for the day. It tempted me to want to hit the guards and keep hitting them until they stopped breathing. The Japs didn't give us any water for bathing either, so I would just stand in the rain every day and take my shower that way.

I had never experienced dysentery before and it proved very rough to watch my buddies bent over with the agonizing pain it caused. It was a horrible sight to behold: men, unwashed, unshaven, and in pain, crawling towards the latrine but not having enough energy to even reach it. Once afflicted the men lost their strength, appetite, weight, and even hope or desire to live. They wouldn't even speak or listen to their buddies. I tried to speak to some of the ones that had the more severe cases, but they would not listen to me or even utter a word. It appeared as if they were in another world, becoming nearly helpless in the later stages of the sickness.

It was hard seeing my buddies lying on the ground reduced to skeletons. It was even tougher seeing the bodies of the dead covered with vermin, excreta, and flies lying alongside the open ditches we had to use as latrines. Tears flowed. I never saw any medicine all the while I was at the camp at Cabanatuan, and can only blame the Japs for all of this suffering. I consider myself very fortunate; although having had a very severe case of diarrhea, my condition wasn't as serious as the victims of dysentery.

Everyone had only the clothes they wore, and because it was so damn hot these were permeated with sweat and dirt, which did little to help those suffering from dysentery. If we had had water for washing our clothes there would have been no doubt that we would have done so. Each man had only one dish, and without water there was no way of keeping it clean either. I used to scrub mine with sand to clean it as best I could.

A buddy of mine from my Shanghai days, Jack Taylor, was also in Cabanatuan. Jack had been in the Marines for twenty years and knew his way around. He was able to make a lot of friends in the camp and somehow came up with several cans of canned food, which he divided with me. I will never forget the advice he gave me. "Ed," he said, "never give up regardless how tough the situation gets, hold your head high and fight." When I left the camp Jack was still there. I never saw him again and often wonder if he made it back. I am always hoping that one day soon I will meet big Jack at one of the American Defenders of Bataan and Corregidor conventions. [Ed never again mentions meeting Jack, and, unfortunately, the author could not find any additional reference to him.]

After about three months of just sitting around the camp and, being hungry all the time, thinking about food and water, I soon became bored. I never did like the onion soup and rice they served us either, not that they served us much of it. It was about that time that I heard rumors that the Japs were going to send us on work details elsewhere in the Philippines. In describing these new rumored work details the Japanese used the now familiar ruse, "*Shigoto tocson, messy tocson,*" which meant, "Work very hard and you get very much chow." I began to think about my future, how long this war would last, how long I would stay in this camp, and what was happening back home with regards to the war effort. I realized that if I stayed here in this camp under these existing conditions indefinitely it would be really rough on me, both mentally and physically. But I figured that if I went out on a work detail I would get more food and plenty of water. I've always believed that opportunity only happens once, so I decided that when the opportunity arrived I would accept one of the work details.

Several days later a notice was posted on the bulletin board asking for volunteers to go down south to work on an airfield. The bulletin promised good food, good living conditions, and excellent working conditions. I didn't fall for this promise completely, although I did think I might get more and better food because I knew the Japs wanted their airfields built and thought they'd feed us better to give us more energy to build them. The Japanese were looking for 300 good men willing to work, and they were able to fill this quota very quickly. I didn't have much to pack, just my toothbrush and the shorts, shoes, and socks that I was wearing. I was happy to be leaving Cabanatuan; by this time the death toll among the prisoners there was a hundred each day.

This time the travel was different. We rode in trucks to Manila. On our return trip to the capital the Filipinos again gave us the "V" sign for victory, which made us feel somewhat better. They too evidently believed that eventually we would return to liberate the islands. The trip took us about three hours to reach the city. Once there it appeared as though the Japs were everywhere we looked.

There was no doubt that the Japs used forced, free Filipino labor to work on projects beneficial to the Japanese war effort. I noticed many Filipinos with their horses and cars hauling goods to the pier where several transports were being loaded with supplies to be shipped to the many islands where the Japs maintained contingents of troops. There was also no doubt that the Japs were attempting to build the city of Manila, which contained the largest docks in the Philippine Islands, into a fortress.

The trucks we were riding in took us directly to the docks. It's my believe that the Japs didn't want us to notice the many different types of warships in the harbor thinking we might get riled up, so with shouts of "*Hiako, hiako,*" meaning faster, faster, and prods from their bayonet-fixed rifles we were hurriedly loaded onboard an old, rusty looking transport. Just as soon as the last man entered the hold, the hatch door was closed, surrounding us in pitch darkness. When several of the men quickly began loudly objecting to the closing of the hatch, knowing it would soon get very hot inside, the it was immediately reopened and a Jap guard pointed his automatic rifle at us and, as he pulled back the slide on his weapon, yelled, "*Kiotski, koodo, koodo.*" We instinctually took this to mean shut up, which we did. The hatch was again closed, and within an hour, as predicted, the hold became extremely hot and stuffy. The ship didn't get underway for what seemed like hours, but we didn't gripe again, not after that threat with the automatic rifle.

Assuming the Japs would open the hatch once the ship was out of sight of Manila, we were happy when the old transport finally left the dock and headed out to sea. Just as we thought, soon after leaving port the Japs opened the hatch cover and motioned us to come topside. They didn't have to motion to us twice.

The situation had changed completely. Although their English was very limited, all the guards smiled and engaged in conversation with us. They tried their best to be friendly. The sun was shining and they indicated that we could lie and relax on the deck. This was all a complete reversal of the treatment we had received thus far from any of the Japanese since being taken prisoner. The treatment was so different that I began thinking, "What the hell is happening here." Here, onboard this ship, we were being served tea with a slice of lemon, and not five days ago the Japanese were beating the hell out of us with their rifle butts. Just a few days ago the faucets were purposely turned off before everyone had his one cupful of water a day. And here, onboard the old transport, the Japs gave us all the rice we wanted at mealtimes, and the soup was not only flavored with curry, it also contained meat.

I spent the trip relaxing on deck until it got too hot during the day. I would then slip back into the hold to get out of the sun. I was really at a loss to explain the treatment we were receiving onboard. I thought that our little yellow friends must have had some type of ulterior motive; no doubt they were attempting to build up our spirits and expected us to do good work once we arrived at our destination.

Also onboard the old transport were several women, which no doubt satisfied the Japanese guards' sexual desires. The guards also played with pet monkeys they had brought along.

Previous to this trip I would never have dared ask a guard for information, but now, because they were so friendly, I inquired of one as to where we were going. The guard smiled and said, "We go to Palawan and build big airfield, and you like it to work." The whole trip was smooth sailing all the way to our destination, and on the fifth day of our voyage the old transport docked at Palawan. [Port of Puerto Princesa on the Philippine Island of Palawan.[26]]

Almost immediately the situation changed. A different group of guards were waiting.

4 Palawan and McKinley Field – Philippines

The Japanese guards that were waiting for us on the pier in Palawan were evidently from the airfield that we were sent to build and were to be our guards and supervisors in the building of the airfield during our stay on the island. The first words they uttered to us were the familiar *speedo, speedo, haiko, haiko* as they prodded us to quicken our movements in offloading both the equipment and ourselves from the transport. The equipment and tools we would be using to build the airfield were lifted from the ship by a hoist. The hoist, however, didn't reach all the way to shore. So we had to wade out into the water and carry the equipment the rest of the way. The water was damn near up to our necks and it was a struggle to lift the heavier equipment. Only after several falls and much difficulty did we finally manage to get it all to shore.

We were then marched to a small village nearby, which consisted of about a hundred thatched huts. A thick jungle of tall grass and several varieties of trees, including coconut, banana, and lime, along with a few other types, surrounded the village on all sides. I was informed that when the Japanese arrived they just told the natives living in the village to leave, and the Japs just moved in.

To my surprise we were moved into a barracks formerly occupied by the local constabulary police. It had a good roof that didn't leak and a wooden floor on which we spread our blankets. Next to the barracks was an empty field. On one side of our camp were the huts that the Japanese guards lived in, and a heavy wire fence surrounded the entire camp up to these huts.

That first day at Palawan the camp commander, Lieutenant Yamagota, had the 350 of us in the work detail line up on the field next to our barracks for an introductory speech. Once we were all lined up, he yelled out a loud *kiotskiiiiii*, purposely drawing out the *iiiii* to call us to attention. With everyone standing at attention, the lieutenant pointed to the jungle and spoke to us stating that we were going to build an airfield where the jungle was marked off. He stated that we would have to *shigoto* (work) very hard and we would have *tocson komay* (very much rice) to eat. He then warned that we would be shot if we attempted to escape and that we should obey all of the rules made by the Japanese guards because the rules were fair and equitable. He ended his speech by stating that we were working for the Emperor, adding that each morning and night at formation we were to bow our heads and pray to the Emperor. I can tell you that this is one thing that we did not go for one bit. We did have to bow to the East, but our guards couldn't hear what we were saying about their Emperor over the loud prayers of the Japanese troops, and I can assure you that I cussed the Emperor every morning and night while bowing at *bango*.

Each morning at 6:15 a.m., and again in the evening at 7:30 p.m., we were assembled on the parade ground for *bango*. Counting in Japanese from one to twenty went as follows: *ichi, ni, san, shi, go, roku, shichi, hachi, ku, ju, juichi, juni, jusan, jushi, jugo, juroku, jushichi, juhachi, jukyu, niju*. Throughout my time as a POW I was assigned several different numbers, a different one at each camp—none of the numbers being the same. In some camps I was assigned a specific number, in others I was not. At Palawan, as in Manila, I was not. While in the camp in Japan, however, my number was 475 (*shi shichi go*).

Our first meal at Palawan was the same as those in the Philippines, a dish of *lugao*—as before, so watery you could actually drink it—and soup similar to the millet soup but with a different type of weed; a weed too coarse to enjoy. They also served us tea that was so thin we could actually see the bottom of the old fifty-gallon gas drum it was made in.

The guards selected prisoners to be on guard duty every night in the camp. These prisoner-guards were to be on the lookout for fires and escaping prisoners. If a prisoner escaped at night, the prisoner-guard on duty at the time would be held responsible. In addition, a guard shack was positioned directly across the road from our barracks housing a machinegun and twelve Japanese guards armed with bayonet-fixed rifles. These guards sat on chairs and, never seeing them move except during the guard changes, they appeared to always be very alert. During the nights I occasionally would hear these guards barking out commands as their shifts where changed; no doubt to let us know they were still there.

At about 6 a.m. each morning our Japanese guards walked through the barracks shouting, "*Bango, bango,*" hitting the wooden floor with their gun butts to get us up. Ten minutes later we were expected to be out on the parade ground for count off. After the *bango* a Japanese sergeant would command everyone to lower his head and pray to the Emperor. We would then wash up for breakfast and have our bowl of watery rice and weak tea. I didn't know how in the hell they expected us to *shigoto* digging, chopping, and shoveling, all of which required hard labor, all day long in the jungle on that diet.

At 7 a.m. we were marched to the jungle. There, the tools—axes, saws, picks, shovels, grub hoes, and crosscut saws—were all neatly lined up waiting to be used. The Japs had a rule that at quitting time we had to completely wash clean whatever tools we used during that day. On the first day at work at Palawan a Jap sergeant explained to us just where he wanted us to work, showing us the stakes which had been placed every fifty feet on either side of the site. Our first big job was to saw down the large coconut trees, many of which were two feet or more in diameter. It took two men to use the crosscut saws, so we usually worked in pairs on these trees.

I soon discovered that many of the men on the detail had never before used such a tool as a crosscut saw. I found it very hard to work with these men, so I always tried to find someone who had worked on a farm before, because they were more familiar with the tools that we used and proved to be better workers. A number of the men, likewise, especially those from the cities, had never before had an axe in their hands. Accidents were bound to happen, and they did. During my stay at the camp quite a few of the men were hurt, several cutting themselves with axes, a few others breaking their arms. Not surprisingly, most of these injuries were caused by the inexperience of the man working with the tools and by not using good sense while using them.

Working on the airfield was a hell of a lot of work. Each coconut tree had about a million roots, and the only way to get them out was to dig a trench about six feet away from the trunk to expose them. We would dig this trench about fifteen inches deep all around the entire tree and then chop off most of these exposed roots. The whole process took my partner and me about five days to finish one tree: one day to saw down the tree and cut the large limbs off, three days for digging and chopping the roots, and one day to cut up the small limbs and trunk. We also had to carry everything to a pile where it would later be burned. The next step was to carry away rocks and fill in the holes and low spots on the airfield. We had the use of wheelbarrows to help us with this. The rains would make the field a muddy mess, so when it rained I would tie a rope around my waist and pull our wheelbarrow as if I were a horse. After the low spots and holes were filled in, the process of felling trees would begin all over again.

Although by 8:00 a.m. each day the sun would be hot and perspiration poured from our bodies, there was never such a thing as a break for a smoke or a drink. Working in pairs, we would take turns with one man working on a rough job for an hour and then switching to a lesser strenuous one, such as trimming the smaller branches for an hour. I had only been in Palawan several days when I realized that it wasn't hard to comprehend that the Japs were not going to win this war by building airfields with picks and shovels.

We would work from 7 a.m. until 12 noon, at which time we would be lined up for a *bango*. The Japanese didn't want to loose much time so they brought our lunch out to the field. After our *bango* we ate the lunch, which consisted of a small ration of rice, some of the strange green weed soup, and the light colored, tasteless tea. By 12:30 p.m. we were back on the airfield working again.

At 5 p.m. the work ended for the day. We would carry our tools used that day to an open area and wash each one until it was entirely free of dirt. A guard checked every tool, okaying each to insure the tools were clean. We would then line up for another *bango*, after which we'd march back to the camp where we washed up for dinner. Served at 5:30 p.m., our dinner consisted of the same meal we had for lunch. About every other week, however, and although it was only about the size of one good bite, we were given a piece of fish with our dinner.

Each day before starting work I spent a good deal of time searching my work area for any of the huge 4-inch circumference black snakes that we encountered. These large snakes were always on my mind while working in that jungle. The grass was so tall you couldn't always see them, and they hid in holes and tree stumps. Whenever one of these snakes would appear I would call to one of the men who were from one of the southern states, and they would come and kill it for me. The Japanese guards allowed us to eat anything we caught, and if one of the bond fires of tree stumps and branches were burning we would cook the snake over the fire and eat it.

For about the first two hours of each morning the tall jungle grass was wet, and each morning my shoes got soaked, causing them to begin to rot. After about a month of this they actually rotted right off my feet. Unfortunately, the Japs didn't have shoes large enough to fit me at that time. Whenever I asked, all they would say was, "We get you shoes very soon." However, it wasn't for another eighteen months and three airfields later that I received a replacement pair of shoes.

It was really rough for me from then on in Palawan. Darn near every day my feet bled from the sharp and craggy rocks I was constantly stepping on; the guards only laughed and muttered to themselves at my predicament. The underbrush was very thick in the Palawan jungle, and in it was plenty of thistle-type weeds. Each time I stepped on one of these thistles the needles would penetrate my feet. If I sat down to remove the needles, the guards would yell their *speedo, speedo*. There were many times when the guards laughed at my bleeding feet that I lowly muttered to myself, "You dirty sons-of-bitches, I would like to kill you and just hope I get the chance." If they had heard me, I know they would have killed me right then and there, but I had my mind made up that I wasn't going to let those little yellow bastards get me down.

The Japanese guards assigned to the work details at Palawan were very tough, especially after several escapes. Throughout our imprisonment in the Japanese POW camps we were always in threat of being beaten, sometimes for little or no reason at all. In Palawan many of these beatings were administered because a man, hungry, was caught stealing some limes or coconuts. On the way to and from the airfield we were building we would break ranks to steal a few limes. We knew they would catch us, but we were hungry and didn't care. The usual punishment for stealing limes was a gun butt to the forearms. I am convinced that there are still some men walking around today with crooked arms because of being hit in their forearms with Japanese rifle butts.

The punishment for stealing coconuts was different. One of the punishments was being tied to a flagpole in the morning and left in the hot sun until after it went down. I remember seeing a few men lying as limp as rags at the base of the flagpole after being tied there all day, their whole body burnt, almost as red as a beet. Some of these men were unconscious, requiring several hours to come out of the shock. Several took so long to regain consciousness that the rest of us didn't think they'd make it through the night. Every one of them was completely dehydrated after their ordeal at the flagpole and within a few days their burnt skin would begin to fall off. One man's back was so burnt that it was almost cherry red, he couldn't lie on it for several days. Another man's lips were burnt so bad that the cracks in them were a sixty-fourth of an inch wide and bleeding. He couldn't eat any solid food for about two days. We managed to get some coconuts and gave him the milk to drink so he was able to survive for those two days. All the men, however, regardless of their condition, still had to go back to work on the airfield the next day after their punishment.

Other times when caught stealing coconuts the prisoners were just beaten. I will never forget the night I heard a lot of noise and screaming when the Japanese guards caught several men stealing coconuts stored in a building adjacent to our quarters. I didn't much like listening as the Americans yelled in pain while five or six guards worked them over just because they were hungry and stole a few coconuts. If we had received sufficient food during the days we would not have tried to steal any of the coconuts, limes, or sugar during the nights.

Several months of this harsh treatment and beatings caused men to have wicked dreams. While I walked to the latrine at night I could always hear men cry out in their sleep. Besides the beatings, the work itself, along with the lack of nourishing food, also began having their toll on us.

By the time we had cleared about a 100-foot long section for the airfield the rains began to make the clearing really muddy. Without any shoes to provide for traction I did a lot slipping and sliding around in this mud and my feet soon became very sore—there was nothing that could be done to relieve the pain. The constant wetness from the rains was also slowly killing me.

Besides my sore feet and constantly being wet, the hard, steady work itself, along with the constant heat, also had an effect on me. The temperature during the day ranged from around 100 to 108 degrees, and we didn't have anything covering our heads to protect us from the hot sun. This heat caused many of the men, including myself, to have dizzy spells. Many were the days that between the heat and the sun blaring down on my unprotected head I became dizzy and had blurred vision. If anyone fell over in a faint the guards would just yell their typical *koodo, koodo*, telling the person to stop loafing and get back to work. Thinking a prisoner was faking usually resulted in the tactic of using the gun butt first and asking questions later. Sometimes, though, a prisoner would get better attention if he just fell over; this happened on occasion.

Our camp's American doctor didn't play fair with all of us, and probably had his favorites. As it was, it didn't do any good to go on sick call if you could still walk. If you were able to walk into sick call the American doctor just grinned at you and said, "Next man." And if you became sick anytime before the morning sick call you still had to wait until sick call; there were very few exceptions to this. It seemed as if one literally had to be on the verge of dying to get put on the sick list and stay in the camp.

I was soon getting thinner, which wasn't bad, but I also started having a steady cough. It turns out that I had developed pleurisy [an inflammation of one or both membranous pleura sacs lining the thoracic cavity and enveloping the lungs] in the left side of my chest, which really began to get me down. Every time I took a swing with a grub hoe, pick, or axe my left side ached badly. It became so bad that I couldn't even take a deep breath. I don't know whether the doctor gave a damn or what, but he never let me stay in camp and I had to continue working on the airfield, all the while suffering from pleurisy. I struggled along for about three months this way, experiencing severe chest pains each time I lifted one of our tools over my head in order to get a good, powerful swing. When I complained to either the American doctor or the Jap guards they only laughed.

Pleurisy wasn't the only sickness among the POWs at Palawan. The island was about the heaviest mosquito infested of all the Philippine Islands, and as a result numerous prisoners suffered from malaria and dengue fever [an infectious tropical disease transmitted by mosquitoes and characterized by fever and severe joint pains.] There was no quinine available, and regardless of how we felt we had to work.

After a hard day of working at the airfield cutting, sawing, and digging we were ready for a shower. But, since there were only two showerheads available in the camp and many of us didn't want to wait in line, we would just stand under the eaves during the nightly rain shower and have our bath. There was, however, one thing wrong with this procedure: the rainwater was too cold and a man could really get chilled. A great number of people might think that a tropical rain is a relief from the heat of the day, but the sudden drop in temperature that comes with the cold rain can be fatal, especially to someone suffering from dysentery. We also soon found that it wasn't good for a person to be perspiring very much and then get chilled, especially if the person had malaria.

One night while relaxing under my mosquito net—surprisingly we actually had mosquito netting for our beds while on Palawan—I began coughing and couldn't quit. After about an hour of this I began gasping for air and had so much difficulty breathing that I realized I was on the way out. Hearing me grasping for air, a buddy said, "What the hell is wrong, Ed?" When I couldn't answer, he quickly called the Japanese doctor, who arrived in a few minutes and gave me two powerful pills and a can of condensed milk. These two pills were very effective and stopped my coughing. The doctor also, right then and there, said "No more *shigoto* on the airfield."

The next morning I was re-assigned from the airfield detail to stand the nightly prisoner-guard duty watching the camp for fires and escaping Americans. Watching for fires I would do, but I wasn't about to prevent any Americans from going over the fence if they thought they could make it through the jungles to freedom.

I will never forget the night eight men escaped while I was on this prisoner-guard duty. It wasn't until *bango* the next morning that the escapees were missed by the Japanese, who immediately sent out a truckload of guards with rifles and machineguns in pursuit. I was hoping the Japs wouldn't find the Americans, but about four hours later the Japs returned with all of the men. The guards lined the escapees up on the parade ground and shot them in sight of the rest of us so all could witnesses the incident. The camp commander, Lieutenant Yamagota, then said the Japanese would not tolerate any escape attempts and that this was to serve as an example of what would happen to any other men who attempted to escape.

Since I had been on prisoner-guard duty the night of the escape I was called over to see the camp commander. My notification of this came when a guard arrived at my shack and escorted me to see the boss. As I entered the camp commander's office a sergeant issued a very loud *kiotski*, to which I responded by standing at attention in front of a large, black, walnut table which the lieutenant used as his desk. Wearing dark sunglasses, Lieutenant Yamagota sat behind this table. I could tell he was very disturbed and angry, and I realized that I was really on the carpet.

The lieutenant began to fire questions and accusations at me in rapid succession, which were relayed to me by an interpreter. "Why didn't you see them?" "What time did they escape?" "Why didn't you try to stop them?" "I think you helped them escape!" I realized he was attempting to corner me and I knew he was angry because he kept pounding his fist on the table. Although I was shaking, I didn't want to allow him to think I was scared, so after he finished questioning me I said that my chest ached and sat down to rest. The lieutenant then scolded me in Japanese for about another two minutes. It sounded like he called me every bad name in the book. Whenever he momentarily paused I replied, "*Hai, hai*," which meant yes, yes, I agree, you are right. Then, just when it appeared as though I would be shot, the interpreter said, "Ok, you may go." I bent my head slightly forward and replied, *"Arigoto,"* (thank you) and returned to my shack. I had made it through the ordeal!

Shortly after the big escape the Japs posted a new regulation on the bulletin board. It stated that if just one man escaped, ten men would be immediately executed. I was very happy that there weren't any more escape attempts during the remaining part of my four-month prisoner-guard duty.

By that time I was living from one day to the next and thought a lot about my parents and brothers and sisters. Many times I've thought that it must have been a miracle for me to have made it through a hell on earth like that. I always said my prayers each night before I fell asleep, praying that I would make it through the next day.

The promise the Japs had made to us at Cabanatuan about *tocson messy* (very much chow) had been just a gimmick to get men to volunteer for work on the many Japanese airfield projects. Along with the poor food ration at Palawan, we also received a cigarette ration of just one cigarette per week per man. I was fortunate with this ration because I didn't smoke cigarettes and would give my ration to a buddy who really appreciated it. What hurt me, though, was that the natives that passed by our shacks were all smoking those good long black cigars, and I would have paid $100 for one, or for a bottle of beer.

At Palawan the kitchen detail was rotated weekly. The detail helped the cooks serve the rice, soup, and tea. I hated being on it because there just wasn't a sufficient amount of any of the food, causing the ration that we had to give each man to be just too damn small. It hurt me to see those thin, emaciated bodies stagger up with their pan expecting, or even just hoping, that I would fill their dish with rice and soup. I really think some thought that if they smiled at me or uttered a few words that I might give them a larger ration, and many of the men thought the servers played favorites. But I always tried to be fair with everyone. A number of times we didn't even have enough food to go around and a few of the men had to go without anything at all to eat.

The leaves and stalks of the vegetable in the soup had a tendency to settled to the bottom of the can causing the majority of the men to receive mostly liquid. Because of this, during the evening meal some of the men would stand in line for fifteen minutes prior to the beginning of the servings thinking that the soup would be thicker at the beginning, while others waited until the line was almost finished thinking the soup would be thicker towards the bottom. After being on the kitchen detail on Palawan,

I know that if we had not stolen the limes and coconuts many of us would not have made it back to the States alive due to the fact that the Japs failed to supply the cooks with enough soup ingredients and rice.

In a way I was lucky that night that I almost died of pleurisy, because four months later I was among twenty-two men who were shipped back to Manila and Bilibid Prison, which the Japs claimed to be a hospital. On the list of men that were shipped back with me were five with dysentery, four with malaria, eight with broken or injured bones caused by on the job mishaps, and five with broken or injured bones resulting from beatings.

When I look back over the years, many times I have felt fortunate to have left the Island of Palawan. Just before the war ended the dirty Japs herded all the prisoners left on Palawan into a cave, built a fire at the entrance of the cave, and suffocated those inside with the smoke. Those that tried to come out were gunned down with machinegun fire. [The Japanese War Ministry issued a POW execution order on 1 August 1944 stating that all POWs were to be killed if they were about to be liberated by Allied forces. Fearing General Douglas MacArthur's forces were about to land on Palawan, on 14 December 1944, the Japanese herded all the remaining POWs working on the airfield at Palawan, all of which were Marines, into air raid shelters. Gas was poured into the entrances and then set on fire. Most of the Marines that tried to escape were bayoneted or gunned down by rifle and machinegun fire. Of the 150 Marines that were herded into the air raid shelters that day, only 11 managed to escape and find their way back to the Allied lines.[27]]

The trip back to Manila also served another purpose for the Japanese. After arriving in Manila and offloading us, the ship returned to Palawan with a load of healthier prisoners and more tools and equipment to speed up the construction on the airfield. I imagine they also took rice and a good supply of weeds or some type of vegetable that no one else wanted to add to the soup for the men at Palawan.

At Bilibid Prison I was assigned an old cot to rest on, which was located on the second floor of a concrete building. While at the prison I received a small ration of rice and soup each day, but I didn't work. It is my opinion that the Japs wanted the Red Cross to think the Japanese were trying to save lives with medical treatment, and therefore called Bilibid a hospital. However, during my approximate one-month stay at Bilibid Prison I never did see a doctor.

While at the prison, I noticed that the Manila harbor was crowded with numerous war ships and transports, and in the city itself were thousands of

Japanese troops. This left no doubt in my mind that the Japs had complete control of the city and the surrounding islands. In my heart, though, I knew that one day in the future American troops would return and take back all of the Philippine Islands. I also had it in my mind that one day I would return home to Maplewood, Wisconsin, unless the Japs shot me.

One day, after about a month of resting at the prison, a Japanese sergeant came by my cot and said, "You come here, tomorrow you go to *shigoto* on airfield." At 7 a.m. the next morning about fifty of the men who had been injured on Corregidor and Bataan, or, like me, on work details, began a march, although we didn't travel too far. After only about an hour of marching we reached our destination, McKinley Field.

We didn't do much work on the actual airfield itself while we were there, but did dig a large amount of trenches around the field and main buildings. We also constructed gun positions at the field; the Japs must have been expecting to receive air raids soon. It hurt my pride to have to build bomb shelters for the Japs and I tried not to cooperate too well—but I really had no choice. I can tell you this, though; the bomb shelters weren't constructed to withstand any bombs.

As usual, the heat was a factor at McKinley Field with the temperature always hovering between about 98 and 105 degrees. The food was the same as at both Cabanatuan and Palawan—too little of everything and not enough of anything—and we worked from daylight till dark. However, one thing was different at McKinley Field; our captors here were commanded by higher-ranking officers than those at the other camps. I imagine Manila was a headquarters for this part of the Pacific, which probably had something to do with the ranking structure.

A great number of our days at McKinley Field were spent working not at the field, but in the city of Manila where we moved very beautiful furniture from some of Manila's best civilian homes to Japanese offices for the Japs' use as office furniture. The guards urged us along with the usual *speedo, speedo* as they pointed at the fancy tables, chairs, and desks they wanted us to move. The Filipinos watched on in dismay and tears as we loaded the furniture onto trucks. If the Filipinos objected, the Japanese guards brandished their rifles and bayonets and yelled, "*Koodo, koodo,*" telling the Filipinos to shut up and get out of the way. I figured the Japs didn't have it as nice in their own country, so they tried to live like kings at the expense of the Filipinos as long as they, the Japs, were in control. I was sure that one day after the Yanks landed in the Philippines and freed the Filipinos the Filipinos would probably take it upon themselves to kill their share of Japanese.

While at McKinley Field we were also put to work on the Manila docks where we loaded transports with gas, oil, rice, cement, peanuts, and any other items that the Japanese troops could use on the many islands they held. Working on the docks was rough on me because I was barefoot and had to be very careful not to crush my feet. But I, like all the other men working on the docks, wanted to work there because there was always the chance of stealing a few hands full of brown, deliciously tasting sugar. We also managed to get an occasional coconut or a little tea while working there.

Several times the dirty bastards [Japanese guards] would allow us to take peanuts, which we did, filling our pockets with them. Then, when we returned to camp, the guards would pull a shakedown, strip us of our peanuts, and then beat the hell out of us with their bayonet butts.

The fact that three or four guards would take turns slugging me during my many beatings didn't bother me too much. They seemed to get a kick out of taking turns hitting me with their fists and watching me fall in pain. But, in reality, I just rolled with the punches and faked being hurt. I enjoyed watching them laugh thinking they had hurt me. [It should be remembered that Ed was a boxer prior to the war and had even taken on heavy-weight champions, and won.]

I thought the brown sugar was the best thing to risk stealing because it made our rice taste so much better, and if I was going to get caught with anything and take a beating for it, I chose it to be for stealing sugar.

All of us were getting very tired from digging and shoveling dirt and working on the docks. Tropical ulcers the size of quarters and half-dollars began appearing on our legs, and the Japs didn't provide anything to heal them.

Around about this time the absence of foods containing vitamins necessary in keeping the body adequately supplied just to maintain the strength to survive began to show its effect on myself as well as every one of my buddies. I noticed my mouth had become very raw in the palate area, and my pelvic area was red and sore. In addition, my testicles became as red as cherries. We all appealed to the Japanese camp commander telling him that if these conditions became intolerable we wouldn't be able to work. To relieve the raw and itchy feeling the Japs took some old fifty-gallon gasoline drums, filled them half full of water, and added some sort of chemical or medicinal compound. Every night we all took turns soaking in the barrels. Although this soaking process continued almost all night in order to accommodate the approximately 300 men at the camp, it did give us some needed relief.

It was also about this time that a loss of coordination and mental torpor and an unsteady gait began to appear among the prisoners; again a result of the starvation diet and the lack of essential vitamins. On top of all this, my feet became very sore and ached nightly from not having shoes to wear. I didn't complain, though, because I knew the Japs wouldn't have listened anyway. Any time I had attempted to speak to the Japs in the past about such things they had just laughed. And our own American camp leaders weren't any help either; they wouldn't intervene in an effort to secure shoes for me.

Conditions at McKinley Field were truly like a nightmare. Years later when I told my wife about the situation at the camp I told her it reminded me of a train wreck back in the States where a hundred people had been injured and everything seemed in an uproar. Our sleeping quarters at the field were in an old barn where hogs, chickens, and horses had been housed prior to us, and the mess from these animals had not been cleaned up before we moved in. Among other things, this caused flies, which we had to fight off by the thousands. Many of the men were only eighteen to twenty years of age, and a lot of them took their predicament rather hard. The medical conditions affected the nerves of many of these fine young men, all who had already survived the countless long marches and cruel treatments dished out by the Japanese. The constant pain and sick feeling from the sores and illnesses these men were enduring day in and day out made them easily irritated, resulting in many arguments breaking out, arguments that would not ordinarily have happened. This all contributed to the constant crying and moaning that went on throughout the nights, making it a difficult place to get much rest.

Our little Japanese friends had a great many airfields in the area that they wanted to expand to enable them to land heavier airplanes, and they appeared to be in a hurry to complete the project at McKinley Field. Every day it was *speedo, speedo* and the usual prods with the bayonets. But somehow, however, as bad as it was, we managed to survive the terrible ordeal at McKinley Field.

5 Nielsen Field – Philippines

An announcement was made one evening that the next day we would be leaving McKinley Field to work on yet another airfield located just six or seven kilometers away. Some of us began to think that the Japanese thought we had become accustomed to the conditions of hard work with little food and nonexistent medical treatment we had been forced to work and live under these past months, and we thought they figured we would do a better job at the new airfield.

Early the next morning at about 6:30 a.m. the guards yelled their normal *bango, bango, speedo, speedo*, telling us to hurry and line up for the morning count. After eating and drinking our usual *lugao* and cup of tea, by 7 a.m. we were marching down the gravel road. It had begun to warm up by about 8 o'clock that morning and by the time we marched through the gates of our new home, Nielsen Field, I knew it would be another hot day.

Nielsen Field was a much larger airfield than McKinley Field had been, and as such was able to accommodate bigger and heavier airplanes. The camp itself at Nielsen Field was also an entirely different camp than the one at McKinley Field. The shacks we slept in were newly constructed of fresh bamboo, and everything was very clean. A strong, heavy, barbed wire, ten-foot tall fence, topped with several inward-slanting strands of wire, surrounded the camp. In addition, large searchlights were situated about every forty to fifty feet along the fence. At night these would light up the entire camp like a city. The compound had only one gate, which was covered with barbed wire and strengthened by iron bars. A guard shack housing a tripod mounted machinegun and manned twenty-four hours a day by twelve guards was positioned ten feet from this gate. The shack I lived in was about twenty-five feet from the gate and in direct line of the machinegun. Like at the camp on Palawan, the guards manning the guard shack continuously sat very erect with their bayonet-fixed rifles always at the ready for action. Every four hours these guards would change shifts under the loud and clear commands of their commanders.

The guards at Nielsen Field proved to be about the most sadistic of any I encountered throughout my days as a POW. It seemed as if the more hatred these guards had for Americans the more sadistic they tended to be. I think many of them wanted to impress their fellow guards, and their way of doing this was by beating on the prisoners.

I believe I understood the Japs better than many of the other men did. I had spent over three years in the orient in Shanghai and the Philippines before the war started, and in viewing the differing oriental peoples during these three years I came to realize that there seemed to be a great deal of similarity between all of them. In the case of the Japanese, I could tell their temperament by the actions and expressions on their faces, and their temperament told me which ones I could trust and which ones I could not. I found that you had to use a certain amount of psychology with the Japanese guards to get along as well as possible with them because each one had a different personality. Many would not say a word to me all day long, while others quite often wanted to talk. Still others would speak only when necessary. A few would slug you if you laughed at them or attempted to speak to them unless they first asked you a question or told you to do a certain job. You could tell the more sadistic guards by the dirty smiles they'd wear on their faces. They would watch you constantly, never smiling at anyone, never engaging in conversations, and never tolerating any talking on the job. We were all glad when a character like that was transferred to different details.

As I've mentioned, everyone, sooner or later during our captivity, would be subjected to beatings with clubs or rifle butts. I think this was especially true there at Nielsen Field. Every day while working on the airfield at least one man took a beating. It hurt to see one's buddies being punished for no apparent reason. I know the guards would have liked to see one of us strike them back, but they always had their bayonet-fixed rifles ready to back them up.

These many beatings eventually caused each of us at one time or another to have violent dreams and nightmares. Every night when I went to the *benjo* (toilet) while at Nielsen Field, I could hear men crying out, "No, no, no!" in their dreams. But I never heard any one of them cry during a beating; they were all so proud to be American that they refused to cry or admit defeat.

I was six feet tall, and when it was my turn to be beaten on, five or six of the short Japs would gang up on me and take turns slugging me. I honestly believe they felt proud because they could beat up on a big American Marine. I would have enjoyed taking on these smart little men about two years back when I was in my boxing shape.

In the evenings, when it was nice and quiet in the shacks and everyone lay sleeping, two or three guards would come marching through. Without warning, they'd suddenly stop, point at a man, and say, "You, come here." The prisoner would then be marched to the guard shack where the these same guards would proceed to beat him with pick handles, all the while telling the camp commander that the man hadn't worked hard enough during the day. I couldn't see the legitimacy in this because if a man didn't work hard enough on the airfield during the day the Japs would just beat him right then and there on the spot.

The camp commander was a Japanese lieutenant. He was of slender build and wore dark sunglasses. We named him "Mickey Mouse." He had several sergeants, plus some lower ranking one, two, or three star privates. The lower ranking guards, the privates, were the most wicked. They always carried their bayonet-fixed rifles, which seemed to make them feel big, and these privates would strike us at the slightest provocation; many times it wasn't called for. I believe they wanted to make points with their sergeants and camp commander, and beating us was a way for them to do it.

To illustrate what type of guards we had at Nielsen Field, let me mention an incident that happened. Ten of our men received permission from the camp commander to put a show on during one of our days off. Five of the guards attended the show and enjoyed the dancing and singing of our men. Everyone was happy for a half an hour after the show, when all of a sudden six sturdy guards came into the compound and escorted the ten showmen to the guard shack. One of the guards shouted, "*Kiotski*," to which the ten showmen stood at attention not realizing exactly what was about to happen. Each guard then picked up a pick handle and, as each of the showmen stepped forward, each of the guards hit the man five to six times in the rear with the pick handles. The guards swung their pick handles from left field and each man's buttock was busted and bleeding. Some of these blows landed in the prisoners' kidneys, causing the man to fall to the ground. When this happened, a pail of water was thrown over the victim. All of this happened right in front of the fence by my shack.

This was a cowardly act; the dastardliest that I had seen up to that time and strictly uncalled for. Many of us were really hot, and I can guarantee you that if the Japs had not had weapons we would have beaten the hell out those dirty little yellow skinned bastards. Those guards should have been punished; the Japs should not have been permitted to get away with such tactics.

Like at other camps, our doctor at Nielsen Field didn't have much to treat the men with, and all he could do was put methiolate on the bruises and cuts and cover them with cotton, gauze, and tape. At 7 a.m. the next morning the ten showmen were lined up ready to go to work. There was no doubt their buttocks were still sore as hell, but all the same, they all still worked a full day. I tell you, it took courage to do what those men did for us. I have much praise for every American who stood up without a wince, and I bet the Japs never thought the Americans were so tough.

Several times a week at this airfield camp the guards would practice bayonet fighting on their side of the fence, directly opposite of my shack; no doubt just to impress us. They always made unnecessarily excessive noise as they charged at one another. In my opinion they weren't as good as they wanted us to believe. Watching them made me wish it was two years back, I would have liked to face one of them with a bayonet; I would have pierced him several times and enjoyed watching him die.

Like we had named the camp commander Mickey Mouse, we also gave names to the different guards to identify their type of character. "The Angel" was tough, "The Killer" was capable of doing it, "Moto" was mean, "Shorty" was a very likeable man, "Pistol Pete" was inclined to use his rifle, and "Saki Sam" had too much Saki the night before. The "Beast" was very rough, "The Devil" was very dirty…and I mean he would really punish you. "The Fox" we could never be sure what he'd do, so he could never be trusted, "The Mouse" was a little man that we didn't have to worry about, and "Yamamoto" always dressed very well, like the Admiral he was named after. These characteristics really describe the guards to a "T" and were important for us in knowing how to satisfy the particular guard during our fifteen-month stay there at Nielsen Field.

The camp itself consisted of four shacks for us to sleep in, each having space for 125 men. Each shack was twenty feet wide and had a six-foot space on either side for sleeping, allowing each of us about eighteen inches wide of space in which to sleep. The space in the center of the huts was used for our morning and evening *bango*. It also contained tables for eating our meals. The meals themselves were the same as at all the other camps, watery *lugao* and millet soup. A detail from each shack would carry the rice and soup from the mess shack to our sleeping quarters and later return the empty cans to the mess shack where they would also wash them. Our beds were made of hard bamboo slats, which didn't at all induce any type of sound-sleeping habits. Each prisoner had a blanket to spread on his bed; we used our shorts for pillows. I would end up twisting and turning all through the night on these hard slatted beds, nearly constantly switching from my back to my right side to my left side to my stomach and then back again.

Our shacks were divided into sections of men. Each section was supposed to keep its part of the shack clean, and four men in each section would take turns hauling the meals of rice and soup in cans from the cook shack to our shack where the food was then divided into equal rations for the men. I was appointed a squad leader for the section I was in. As squad leader my job was to try and prevent trouble in the shack. We had more fights between the men at this camp than at any other camp, which proves to me that there was a lot of dissatisfaction among the men, mainly due to the food and the brutal treatment by the guards. An important point to remember is that each man was tired, hungry, and weak, and tempers were very short.

At the slightest provocation a man was ready to fight, and there were many times when it was difficult to stop the men once they started fighting because they were always so angry. We all agreed that if two men insisted on fighting the best thing for the rest of us to do was to just let them go at it. It was the best way to get rid of any quarrels and unload the pressure that built up inside them, and once the fight was over, so were the grudges. As a squad leader I would became the referee just to insure the fights were fought fairly. To tell the truth, though, everyone was too weak to hurt each other, therefore no one ever really got hurt during any of these brawls.

Even so, we didn't want the Japs to hear about any of the fights because the Japs didn't want any trouble that might lead to additional problems for them. If trouble did occur in our shacks, the guards would come in shooting and kill anyone caught fighting that didn't stop immediately. As I already mentioned, by this time I had gotten to know my captors pretty well and could understand their actions somewhat easily, and it wasn't hard for me to understand that for the benefit of all concerned the Japs just couldn't allow the prisoners to fight.

Being a squad leader at times meant trouble, though, because some of the men that I had known before the war tried to play on our past friendships. One of the men, a very good personal friend of mine, was a bit lazy or possibly just wasn't feeling very well; although, if he wasn't feeling well, he didn't tell me so. I was depending upon him to do his part of our shack's daily chores, which he didn't do. All of the prisoners were tired, hungry, and weak, which caused tempers to be short—and I was no exception. I came right out and told him that if he didn't do his part I would kill him. The worst part about this is that I meant it. I was sorry later for losing my temper, because as a result the man never said good-bye to me when I left for Japan, which hurt me and would bother me for years to come because I really wanted to talk to him again.

In the camp we would also occasionally have a man who would not take a daily shower. Some of the rest of us would scrub him with sand to help encourage him to begin showering each day.

Almost every day at Nielsen Field a detail of about twenty-five to thirty men were called to go work on the Manila docks to load transports with rice, hemp, gas, oil, or cement, much like we did at McKinley Field. As usual, everyone wanted to go on these details for an attempt to snatch a little sugar or peanuts, or anything else edible. Although it was very dangerous working on the pier barefooted as I was, and though I was still weak from the pleurisy I had contracted in Palawan, I still wanted to work on the docks because I too wanted to get the extra food. In addition, working on the docks meant that I wouldn't have to walk in the mud and water that I had to walk in when working at the airfield or the other alternative work sites.

On one particular day while working on the pier loading barrels of cement onto a barge—the damn barrels weighed about 800 pounds each—one of the barrels rolled on top of my left foot crushing all five of my toes on that foot. There was nothing else to do about it but to sit down and pull out parts of the toenails from my crushed, bleeding toes and then continue to work, which I did. Later that evening, after we returned to the camp, our camp doctor removed the remaining pieces of toenails.

When not working on the Manila piers, we worked on the Nielsen airfield itself. The road from the camp to the airfield was stone, and we walked this stone road to and from the camp four times a day—they would bring us back to camp at mid-day to eat our lunch. Every time I would attempt to walk on the grass alongside the road, trying to protect my sore feet and smashed toes, a guard would always holler, "*Koodo, koodo,*" telling me to get back on the road. If I didn't move fast enough the guard would either prod me with his bayonet or use his rifle butt on my rear. I usually cussed him out in a way he couldn't understand me; if he could have understood me I'm sure I would have been in for a beating.

Without shoes to wear, my toes were really getting sore, and not being able to avoid stepping in water nearly every day, my toes never had a chance to heal. I tried tying rags around them, but the rags would quickly fall off. A buddy made a pair of wooden shoes for me in hopes they would help, but I couldn't walk fast enough in them to keep up with the other men, so I had to continue marching and working barefooted.

While at Nielsen Field I was very lucky in meeting another man from Wisconsin who was a very good worker, always doing his share of work. Being aware of my condition, he even did more than his share at times. [According to Jeanette Babler, this was Clifford Omtuedt from Eau Claire, Wisconsin. Cliff was later a police officer in Eau Claire, and the Babler's and Omtuedt's spent many weekends together after the war.] We worked in teams of two digging dirt and loose rock, placing it into cars, and pushing the cars down the line, dumping their contents about 100 feet away, only to repeat this time after time. [Some of the airfields used mine cars and track taken from mines in the Baguio region of the Philippines. The cars Ed mentions may be these same mine cars.[28]]

As I pushed the cars down the track the damn guards would follow me with their bayonet-fixed rifles saying, "*Speedo, speedo, shigoto tocson, messy tocson,*" all day long, but none of it was true; we didn't get more food for working faster and harder. I continued to stub my toes on the tracks and ties, causing them to bleed and hurt, but I never refused to work; I just wanted to move a bit slower while pushing those damn cars. When I was able to work slower I didn't stub my toes as often. But it was always the same, I could always count on seeing one of those bastards chasing after me with his rifle and bayonet at the ready every time I glanced back, and always yelling, "*Speedo, speedo, hiako, hiako.*"

Many were the times I was going to turn around and attack a guard with my shovel, but my good buddy always managed to restrain me. I know if I would have been in good shape I could have killed any one of the guards and would have enjoyed doing so. But my buddy was right in restraining me; I could never have won in the shape or situation I was in. Regardless, we worked hard all day doing this strenuous work as perspiration poured off our bodies.

One day the Japs suggested we push twenty carloads this way, which we did. Sure as hell, the next morning the Jap sergeant in charge said, "Today you push twenty-one cars," which we did, but it took a lot of extra effort. The next day they wanted twenty-two carloads and yelled their normal *speedo, speedo, koodo, koodo, haiko, haiko* telling us to move faster, and this time they walked down the tracks alongside us prodding us on. We pushed their twenty-two carloads that day, but it took an extra twenty minutes, which entirely upset their time schedule. The next day it was back to twenty-one carloads.

We had to work like hell just to get the twenty carloads a day, and some days it took longer to dig the dirt and rock loose. By gradually slowing our digging a little each day and shoveling a trifle slower we were able to stay at our minimum daily number of cars. I think the Japs finally realized it was impossible for us to get a designated number of carloads every day due to the varying daily conditions at the work site. Although I was surprised that we had, we had won this little battle at Nielsen Field.

The field itself had a lot of layer rock, which required the use of picks, crowbars, and wedges to pry loose. And once pried loose, the pieces were so heavy that it took two men to throw the rocks into the cars. We also had the use of pneumatic drills to loosen up the rock. The use of these drills tended to really take the weight off a man in a hurry. I noticed the men that used them were getting weaker and weaker to the point where their ribs protruded from their chests and their legs and arms became thin and bony, but I think they wanted to show off just a bit and still kept at it. I told them to get off that job, that if they did it for six months or more it would kill them. Unless you were there I don't think you would believe what the human body can stand before it collapses and fails to function.

The sick call rule at Nielsen Field was basically simple: if you were able to walk, then you were able to work. It's my belief the Japs must have told the American doctor how many men he was permitted to leave in camp. This rule sure didn't do my feet any good. As I stated, regardless of the fact that I was barefoot and my toes were bleeding, and regardless of having all five toenails removed from my left foot, I still had to walk in the mud and water all day long, digging, shoveling, and pushing cars. Not surprisingly, as a result, a fungus infected my toes, and they have been effected ever since.

For a time, after I returned home after the war, I just let the fungus grow and finally all the toenails on my left foot began to rot. I was lucky that in Waupun, Wisconsin, where I settled, we had a former Navy doctor who had been in the Philippines during the war. I went to him and inquired whether he knew what I had and he replied, "Hell, I took care of the Navy personnel that contacted the same thing." He would wait until the toenail was rotted and then pull it out. At the same time he would cut out some of the fungus. The doctor practiced in Waupun until 1957 when he returned to the Navy. Then, when my new doctor couldn't control the fungus, I went to the Veterans Administration Hospital in Milwaukee, Wisconsin, and showed the doctors there my toes and asked them to remove my toenails. They hesitated for awhile until I stated that I wasn't leaving until they removed my toenails. After finally agreeing, the doctors were able to get most of the fungi cells, but couldn't get them all because of the amount of bleeding that occurred during the operation. It took three months for my toes to heal good enough for me to finally go back to work. Ever since that operation I have had to visit a chiropodist once a month to have my toenails removed and the fungus cut out in order to keep its growth under control.

At Nielsen Field the constant daily pressures, hard work, cruel and unfair treatment, and insufficient food got to quite a large number of men. I know of several that attempted suicide and about half a dozen or so who deliberately injured their own legs or broke their own arms with our tools in order get themselves placed on the disabled list for the duration of the war. If they were disabled or seriously injured they would be sent to Bilibid Prison in Manila. Many of the men were also suffering from malaria by this time, and, with the supply of quinine exhausted, there wasn't much that could be done for them. I remember borrowing about six blankets to cover a good Wisconsin buddy of mine who was lying on the bamboo slats shivering from a bout of malaria.

There was one day that I was allowed to stay in camp because of my bleeding toes. This day turned out to be one of those days that I would never forget. It was the day a big Japanese officer with cauliflowered ears challenged me to wrestle him. Even to this day I can still see him dressed so smartly and speaking such perfect English, telling me that he had graduated from UCLA and that he was checking on the condition of the various camps. Believe me, I told him what he didn't want to hear. My main point centered on the food, because the rations were too small and the soup terrible. I also went on about how we took a lot of beatings. He said he would look into the situation, although I never noticed any changes afterwards. As far as the wrestling went, I hated to have to do it, but I had to refuse the challenge. You can't realize how much it hurt me doing this, but I was too weak because of my smashed toes. Otherwise, I am sure I would have taken him, especially with the amount of determination I had to beat him.

Another day on my never-to-forget list is the day we were at the pier in Manila loading a transport with rice and beans. We must have handled 5,000 bags that day and I saw a chance to damage a few of them, which we did, breaking several of the bags open as we carried them from the warehouse to the dock. When we filled our pockets with the beans from these bags the guards made no effort to stop us, nor did they shake us down once we returned to our camp that evening, so we were all eagerly anticipating a big meal for dinner that night.

After obtaining permission from the guards, the cooks volunteered their services to cook the beans. When the beans were finished cooking the four designated men from each shack brought cans full of these beans to the shacks and we piled our pans high with them. We were all happy and laughing as we ate our fill. About a half an hour later, however, almost every one of us was lying flat on our backs on the bamboo slats, our hearts pounding loudly. When the doctor was called he talked to the guards, who were laughing, seemingly enjoying the whole incident. They informed the doctor that the Filipinos used the beans we had eaten to feed their ponies. The doctor then told us not to eat anymore of the beans, but just to lie down and rest for about a half an hour when it should all go away. All we ended up getting for our trouble that day was a good scare and a huge bellyache.

Although the separate camps that I lived in and worked at differed in work hours, and some had guards that beat the prisoners more than others, life in the prison camps generally took on a certain routine. At Nielsen Field we would hear the familiar *bango, bango* at 6 a.m. twenty-nine out of thrity days, telling us to get up. I would then rise, wash my face with a dash of cold water, and wait for my ration of *lugao* and weak, lukewarm tea, which was expected to enable me to work like hell digging dirt and rock until lunch time. After breakfast we would be marched off to the airfield and work until noon when we would be marched back to the camp for our lunch. Lunch again consisted of some *lugao*, sometimes served with its share of a few crawling insects, and a pan of hard millet soup, the millet always being hard to swallow. Then it was back to the airfield for an afternoon of the same hard work as in the morning.

The 30th day was a day off to wash our clothes. I didn't wear a shirt and, still not having any shoes to wear, I also didn't have any socks. This left me with only a pair of shorts to wash, the one and only pair I wore for several months.

One night, after several months at Nielsen Field without any type of meat, I noticed some hair on top of the soup. Sure as hell, it turned out to be the dog that had been running around the camp. If a man didn't know what it was he probably would just eat it without asking any questions, and several of the men actually liked dog meat after it was fried up.

As a diversion while at Nielsen Field, several nights a week my buddy from Wisconsin along with another friend from Chicago and I would sip tea and shoot the bull in our shack until the guards would holler, "*Shoto*," telling us lights out, time to hit the sack. My Wisconsin buddy was very adept at making deals with a few of the Jap guards, which is how we managed to have tea at night. The three of us always had a lot in common to talk about because we knew about the same happenings in Chicago, Illinois, and Milwaukee and Green Bay, Wisconsin. Being from the mid-West, we discussed different incidents that had happened there prior to our entering the service.

One day my Wisconsin buddy and I were working on the Manila docks loading gas drums aboard a transport [probably a type of alcohol used at the time in some vehicles in place of gasoline]. We decided to have a little party that night because we thought it might have been close to one of our birthdays. We filled two canteens with gas, and, along with a few limes my buddy had connived from a Filipino, after dinner that night we sat alongside the shack and mixed drinks. We had a good time talking about how we played basketball in high school. It was fun to talk about some of the wild times we had had, and for a while we seemed to forget all about being behind the wire fence. The guards watched us while we sat, drank, and laughed, but since we behaved quite well they didn't bother us.

About two hours later we began to feel the effects of the alcohol and, upon becoming dizzy when we stood, thought it best to stop drinking. We both staggered into our shack, began feeling sick, and fell onto our bamboo slats. As soon as we hit the deck we both began to heave. Our buddies noticed our predicament and helped us to the *benjo* at the rear of the shack. My head began whirling around and I became dizzier than hell. My buddy was in the same condition. We spent most of the night with our heads over a hole heaving until we were rid of the alcohol in our stomachs. About every half hour one of the guards would come by to check on us. Our friend from Chicago told the guard that we were *bioki* (sick) from the soup we had for dinner that evening; a statement the guard apparently didn't have any trouble believing because he knew the millet soup was terrible.

We made it through the night and, although the next morning we had a couple of very big headaches, we were able to drink some of the *lugao*, since it was always watery enough to actually drink, and keep it down. Nonetheless, headaches and all, we marched out with the rest of the gang and began digging dirt and rock at the field. That day was a mighty long one, especially when the hot sun hit us.

Why did we get drunk? We lived from one day to the next in the camps and didn't know what the next day was going to bring. So it just felt good to enjoy ourselves for a little while.

On one of the nights at Nielsen Field I made my bed next to a buddy of mine whom I had worked on the Manila docks with. [According to Jeanette Babler, this buddy was James Carrington.] He was from New Orleans and we all called him Frenchy-the-Cajun. As we lay there talking he reached under his blanket and pulled out a black rubber .45 Colt. It was an exact replica of the real .45 caliber automatic handgun. He had a lot of guts to bring it into the camp. How he managed to do so, risking his life in doing it, I don't know, because I never did ask him. I was hoping, though, the Japs wouldn't discover the replica gun because if they did they would surely shoot him. Later, when he was transferred to Bilibid Prison, he was somehow able to escape and ended up fighting with the Philippine guerillas. He really displayed great bravery and determination and wasn't afraid of the devil. Whatever he did with the guerillas he did for the benefit of his country and he deserves great credit for his efforts. I know he must have been a thorn in the plans of the Japanese. I've seen him at a few conventions [American Defenders of Bataan and Corregidor (ADBC) conventions], but have never talked to him about his experiences after we parted at Nielsen Field.

All of the men at the Field had a great amount of pride, and not one of them, even the smallest man in our camp, would back down from anyone. I would say that every man in the camp was my friend and there wasn't anything I wouldn't have done for any of them, whether I personally liked them or not. Whenever I saw a Jap punish an American I hurt inside because I realized that if an American did anything out of line it was due to that person's physical or mental state, which the Japs were responsible for.

I remember my stay at Nielsen Field as one of the roughest I experienced during my captivity. The incidents occurring there cannot be forgotten. Each day that I was there I realized that my chances for survival lessened. The food was no good—the rice rations were too small, the millet soup was too hard to eat because of the hard stalks it contained—the work was extremely hard, the guards were of the roughest kind and insured a large number of the men took the most severe of beatings, and I was still barefoot.

I know many people would disagree with me, but I know that a lot of the food we needed while at the field was available, but was never given to us. I personally saw hundreds of hogs die unused because the Japs just didn't give a damn. There were also hundreds of mules available. I saw a variety of fruits throughout the Philippines that could have been used by us—coconuts, bananas, and mangoes—go to waste rotting on the ground. This fruit, if in our diet, would have prevented the ulcers, beriberi, and raw testicles, and the insides of our mouths wouldn't have been sore, all of which would have helped a man's outlook and made him happy for at least a time.

I believe that the harsh treatment and small rations were designed to get us down to a level of weakness so we could be easily disciplined and wouldn't have sufficient strength for any type of organized resistance. In many ways I believe the Japs were stupid by their violation of the rules of the Geneva Convention because they could have really enhanced their prestige in the eyes of the world, their captives, and their own people had they been more civilized in treating their captives. [The Japanese Minister of War, General Hideki Tojo, issued a Field Service Code on 8 January 1942 stating how every Japanese, military and civilian alike, were expected to view prisoners of war. The Field Service Code basically stated living the life of a POW was a life without honor, and for the Japanese a life without honor is a life not worthy of existence.[29]]

As in all the camps there were no calendars at Nielsen Field. I was happy for this, though, because I didn't want to know the day, week, month, or year. The time seemed to pass by faster if I didn't. When I look back, I believe the steady work and no loafing was better for me, although it would have been much better if our work day would not have been so long and the food more nourishing, and if they could have found me some shoes.

This time wasn't easy for the Filipinos either. It's my belief that the Filipinos in Manila didn't cooperate 100 percent with the Japanese because of the intense hatred the Filipinos had for the Japs. The Japanese took the Filipinos' women, crops, homes, and, in some cases, their places of business, controlling and using all the big hotels for offices and entertainment. On top of that, I heard that the Japanese forced the Filipinos to work for little or nothing and established a strict curfew that everyone had to obey.

After what I believe to have been about fifteen months at Nielsen Field the preliminary work on the airstrip was done, leaving it at a point that machinery was needed to finish it off, so it was time for us to be moved to another camp.

Ed Babler – 1946

Ed at age 18 – Golden Gloves

1220 Days

Bill Russell, Morgan (First name unknown) and Ed Babler enjoying some American Beer after their repatriation in San Diego in 1945.

Ed and Jeanette.

Ed and Jeanette attending an annual convention of the American Defenders of Bataan and Corregidor (A.D.B.C) in Kansas City, Missouri.

Marines and a Sailor from Golf Company, Marine Forces Reserve in Madison, Wisconsin, perform during the 2000 Veteran's Day and Purple Heart Award Ceremony held at the home of Ed's son, Joe Babler, at Lamartine, Wisconsin.

After the ceremony, Jeanette and her sons Joe (left) and John (right) pose for a picture with Ed's Purple Heart Medal.

1220 Days

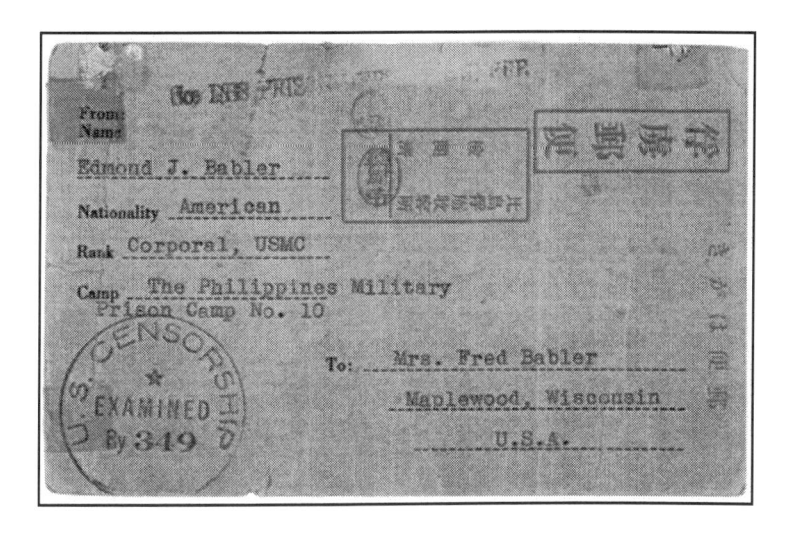

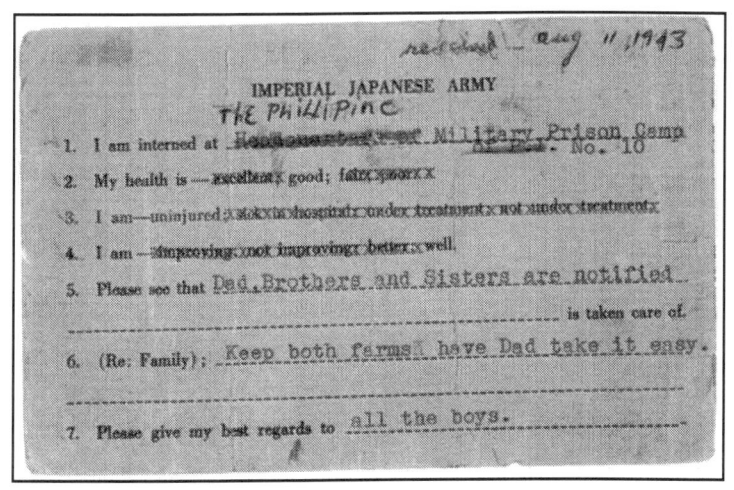

Front and back of one of only three cards Ed was allowed to send in the three years and four months he was held prisoner by the Japanese.

6   Zeblon Field – Philippines

On the day of our departure from Nielsen Field, as normal, the Japs were in a hurry to move out, and at about 6 a.m. we heard the guards hollering their usual *bango, bango, haiko, haiko*, telling us to get up. After eating our *lugao*, drinking our tea, and completing the count we began our march to what would be our new camp, Zeblon Field.

I don't know exactly who made the recommendation, but once we arrived at Zeblon Field I was recommended to work in the cookhouse. I was told there were a lot of rocks on the new airfield site, which would be rough on my feet, so I believe this recommendation was due to that fact. All the men said that I should take the job so I accepted it. After returning to the camp after the first day of working on the new airfield, my buddies told me that it was hell working out there all day long in the hot sun.

My first day at the cookhouse was a rainy one, and it was also slippery. While carrying 200-pound bags of rice the approximately 100-foot distance from a storage shack to the cookhouse, I had to pass over a roughly eight-foot wide drainage ditch. While walking barefoot on the slippery ground it was hard to control the weight I was carrying and I slipped and fell. My left shin hit the edge of a steel plate causing a slice about six inches in length, which began bleeding profusely and giving me a lot of pain. So much so that I told the chef that I had to stop working and went to my shack and lay down on my blanket.

I lie there alone for about an hour; the pain grew more severe and my leg began to swell. I then noticed that a black and blue streak had grown from my shin to my groin area. Within three hours the pain was so severe I could barely stand it and I called to a buddy to get Doctor Hayden, our American doctor. Soon after I began to get dizzy as hell and couldn't move my leg. When Doctor Hayden arrived he took one look at my leg and said, "Ed, I'll have to make an incision immediately to get rid the poison because your leg is infected all the way to your groin." I was getting dizzier all the while and barely remember as Doctor Hayden called over six or seven men to carry me to an old wooden table.

I faintly recall struggling as the doctor was attempting to get my leg ready. The swelling was continuing to grow and the pain became worse. The more the pain increased, the more I squirmed and twisted, and I know I yelled like hell. The last thing I remember before loosing consciousness was seeing the doctor lathering up my leg.

Several hours later I woke to find myself lying on my blanket with my leg, wrapped in gauze, resting about fifteen inches above the ground on top of an old box. My buddies were all waiting for me to wake up; I had a feeling that they hadn't thought I would survive the operation—neither did I. The doctor had cleared most of the poison from my leg with the little medical equipment that he had: a scalpel, gauze, tape, cotton, and some disinfectant. He must truly have had a surgeon's hands because he had to be a real professional to operate in the manner that he did.

The shack I was living in was an old building with hard wooden floors; these same hard wooden floors were used as our beds. I doubled my blanket to form a cushion for my back and used my shorts for a pillow. Every morning, noon, and night two men would carry me to the latrine where they would wash my face and hands, and every few days give me a sponge bath. They were a great group of men. They fed me with a spoon and held a cup of water to my mouth so I could drink. In the evenings after work they would come and talk to me. Every day these same men spent twelve hours working in the hot sun at the airfield. I knew they were tired and hungry, but, nevertheless, they cared for me as if they would have cared for a little baby. What great men we had, and believe me, I know I couldn't have made it without their help.

Every night at about 7 p.m. I went through hell all over again when Doctor Hayden had to clean the wound as it healed. Six men would carry me to the wooden table and hold me down as the doctor used gauze to clean out the poison. Sometimes I was in a daze, but would always awake once I was placed on the table. I can tell you it hurt. The men said I yelled as if I was being killed, and I have no doubt that I did. They told me I was making so much noise that the Japs even came by to see what in the hell was happening. It didn't do any good to complain, so I didn't. Besides, I knew my buddies were going through their own hell each day working on the airfield.

About ten days after my operation the cut had healed, but my leg began to swell again, and with it came more pain. Again I could hardly stand it and my dizziness returned. When Doctor Hayden looked at my leg he told me, "Ed, I will have to make another cut because the infection has extended through your entire leg from one side to the other." Although this was not an ideal situation, I realized that I was in a concentration camp and I couldn't expect anything better. I considered myself lucky, though, to have had such a competent doctor assisted by an able Marine buddy of mine by the name of Louis E. Duncan. I knew I was in good hands with these two. I figured that my number hadn't come up yet since I had come so far, being missed by the shrapnel of hundreds of shells and bombs dropped on me at Cavite and Corregidor and surviving the many beatings I'd already received from my Japanese guards. So, realizing that if Doctor Hayden didn't operate once again I would sure as hell lose my leg, I told him to go ahead.

Once again, six or seven men carried me to the old wooden table. No matter how easily they carried me, as soon as they lifted me off the floor the cut began to hurt and by now the pain was even worse than it had been before the first operation. Before Doctor Hayden made the second incision I was unconscious. When I awoke, I once again found myself lying on my blanket with my leg bandaged up and resting on the box. My buddy told me that the doctor had made a nice cut.

Again, just as the first time, for about five days the wound appeared to be healing fine, but after another few days my leg once again began to swell, this time becoming darn near twice its size. The infection had spread again. Therefore, every night as before, I was carried to the table where Doctor Hayden stuck the gauze under the incision and cleaned out the poison. This cleaning hurt more than the actual cutting. I know that I prayed every night that I would make it through this ordeal, and for about another twelve days I went through the same nightly process: the guys holding me down as the doctor cleaned out the wound. Finally, Doctor Hayden told me that he would have to make another incision; the third.

The third operation went just like the first two—hurting like hell! The men again did a hell of a job of holding me down, and several hours later I awoke lying on my blanket. Upon visiting me and asking how I was doing after this last operation, I replied to Doctor Hayden that I felt much better. He then told me that he believed he did a good job this time. Every day, as before, Doctor Hayden and the men came by to check on me. This time, however, I began to feel better and my leg didn't swell up anymore. After about two weeks I was able to move around by myself and was soon back on the job.

In actuality, except from time to time, I was unconscious throughout the majority of this ordeal, which turned out to be about a six-week period. I never realized what all had occurred while I was unconscious until later when a buddy told me about the care I had received. One man wrote to me several years ago stating that he would never forget the many nights that he helped dress my leg. Another said he knew I went through hell for those six weeks. He said he never thought I'd make it. I really did have a wonderful group of men at this camp, and a day has not passed since my return home that I have not thought about this incident, as well as several other similar ones I would soon encounter on my way to and at Japan.

A few weeks after my last leg operation I told Doctor Hayden that my teeth were hurting. He took a look at them and said that my wisdom teeth had to come out. I told him to go ahead and just pull them, to which he replied that it might hurt a bit. My answer to him was that after what I had just gone through with my leg a month ago nothing would bother me, so he extracted the teeth and I felt better.

"Shorty," as we called one of the guards at Zeblon Field, was about four feet, six inches tall. I was able to establish a good relationship with him, visiting with him on his rounds. Although his English was very limited, we were able to get along quite well. Shorty's name for me was "Big Man," most likely because of my six-foot frame. Since I never wore a shirt, and having quite a hairy chest, he always thought that I was a real he-man. When he came by I would jump at him with outstretched hands, which seemed to make him feel good, and many were the times I had him laughing.

Shorty would come by every day. Whenever he did I would always greet him with *chio* (good morning), and every day we exchanged a few words. After observing his movements each day I think I understood Shorty quite well. It became apparent that he never seemed to look for trouble around the area, and I could have killed him almost anytime in the evenings after darkness set in if I had ever thought of attempting to escape. The fence, though, was well lit, which would have made it difficult to get over without being seen. Because of my relationship with Shorty, however, I was able to have a few extra privileges.

About twenty feet from where I slept there was a bamboo enclosure, and in it were about seventy bags of brown sugar, each weighing about 100 pounds. It must have been intended for us because I had been watching the Jap guards' movements for about four or five weeks and they never took any of it. We had not received any sugar for at least two years and I could almost taste it and certainly could smell it, and I was determined to get some. I realized it would be taking a great risk, because it would mean having to climb over a twenty-foot high bamboo enclosure while guards patrolled the immediate area. I am quite sure that this was in early 1944, because it was around the time when we were seeing American planes again flying over the Philippines.

I assumed the Japs would be more concerned about the planes overhead than worrying about American prisoners trying to escape, so one dark night, armed with a sharp piece of metal and a sack made from a piece of my old overall, I waited until Shorty, who was the guard in the area that night, had made his round of the area buildings.

As soon as Shorty went by, I started to climb over the bamboo enclosure. The bamboo was wet and I slipped back down several times. I finally thought that if I could get my feet wet they would grip the bamboo better, so I soaked them in a puddle and was able to climb up, my wet feet finding the cracks in the bamboo. Only after I was inside the enclosure did I realize the predicament I was in. If a guard came by and checked the number of men in the shack I would have been missed. Although Shorty, the regular guard on this route, wouldn't have checked, others would have. I listened momentarily; it was very quiet. I then quickly slit open a bag of sugar, and with my hands filled my sack. I really worked fast because I wanted to be in and out as fast as I could.

Once my bag was full I waited a few moments before heading back to listen for the sound of a guard. I didn't hear anything unusual except my own heart pounding as loud as I've ever remember hearing it pound. It seemed as though it was making a lot of noise, but in actuality you couldn't hear a pin drop. I waited about another minute until my heart settled down a bit and then began my climb out of the enclosure with my little bag full of sugar. It didn't take long to get back into the camp; the large sugar bags were piled up a few feet from the top of the enclosure, so, after crawling up to the top of the bags, I just let myself hang and drop to the other side.

After safely returning to my shack, I quickly took my bag of sugar and placed it underneath an old shirt that I had hanging on a piece of wire suspended from the bamboo next to my sleeping area. I figured that under an old shirt would be the last place the guards would look. I figured right.

They never looked under my shirt, although they passed by it several times each day. Every day a buddy and I would put a few spoons full of brown sugar on our rice.

In the early part of 1944 I was called over to the camp commander's office. I could only think, "What did I do wrong?" Speaking in very plain English, the camp commander said, "I have some new shoes for you, which you have deserved for over two years." I was really surprised and said, *"Arigoto"* (thank you). He replied that I was welcome, and I saluted him and walked back to my shack. I had waited and suffered a long time without shoes, and I now felt like a little kid who had just been given a new toy. I remember smiling from cheek to cheek and even jumping up and down a few times. This had to be one of the happiest days of my captivity. Realizing that I would probably never get another pair of shoes again as long as I was in captivity, I wiped them off with a rag every night and kept them always as dry as possible.

I recall my buddies telling me that they were really working hard on Zeblon Field because of a rocky ridge that the field was located on. Like at Nielsen Field, a few men were using an eighty-pound jackhammer on this ridge. And just like at Nielsen Field, it took a lot out of a man to use one of these jackhammers; especially with the lack of food we were given. And again, as a result, I remember that one of the men using the jackhammers began losing weight very rapidly. His ribs were soon protruding from his chest and the skin around his body appeared to be really tight, as if it was stretched. In addition, his arms and legs became very skinny. He was a very good worker, however, never seeming to stop to rest. But he could easily kill himself by working too hard to please the Japs, and it wasn't necessary to work that hard. Just like I told the men at Nielsen Field, I told this guy to get off the damn hammer or he wouldn't be going home with us. Unfortunately, I was transferred to a separate camp before I was repatriated and don't know whether or not he ever made it back home to the States.

Our men could certainly have used some steaks while they were working on the airfield. We never got the steaks, though. We did, however, get some horse and mule meat on occasion. Regardless of the fact that horsemeat was sweet, the men really appreciated getting it in their soup and didn't give a damn what kind of meat it was. We also had pork about twice a month, although it wasn't fresh. Nonetheless, when we had meat in our soup, the men were happy.

An unusual situation existed in the camp at Zeblon Field. Evidently the Japs had taken the hogs from the Filipino civilians in the Manila area. There were about 500 of these hogs in an approximately three-acre fenced enclosure located about 100 feet adjacent to our camp buildings. I didn't see one tree inside the large pen, nor were there any shacks to shade the hogs from the sun, and without any shade they suffered from the extreme heat. In addition, the Japs also didn't seem to water or feed the hogs much better than they watered and fed us.

Occasionally, or I should say, often, because of this mistreatment, a hog would be found dead, although the Japs didn't usually see the dead hogs for two or three days. When they finally did see them, the Japs wouldn't eat the hogs themselves but beckoned for me, still on the cookhouse detail, to come over to the fence where they'd throw the dead hogs over and say, "You take it." And I always had to, whether or not I wanted to. By this time the flies had been on them for several days and they didn't smell very well at all, but I would drag the dead hogs to the cook shack and tell the chef that we had another dead hog or two. The chef would shake his head, indicating that he didn't want to risk the men eating something that had lain dead for so long, but a Jap sergeant would always come over to see that we skinned the hogs and served the meat in the soup.

We didn't have any hot water to soak them in, which made it very difficult to get all of the hair off the hogs; so much of it stayed on. Nonetheless, the men were damn hungry, and even when told that the hogs may have been dead for several days the men didn't hesitate to take their ration of soup. In fact, after working all day on the airfield in the hot sun they were actually happy to have the meat in the soup, even meat that may have been bad.

On another occasion, the Japs must have taken several hundred bushels of potatoes from the local Filipinos, because there was a time when we were on a strict potato diet. We had the usual *lugao* for breakfast, but for lunch and dinner it was boiled potatoes along with the millet soup. The potatoes were nearly all starch, very dry, and had no taste, and after about four weeks of eating nearly nothing but these potatoes and our meatless soup twice a day, we soon tired of eating them.

I remember we had a Norwegian in our camp at Zeblon Field. He was caught in Manila when the ship he was on didn't leave the harbor in time. I believe he must have been injured because he stayed in the camp all of the time, never going on a work detail. He took more showers than anyone else, to the point where it seemed as though every time I saw him he was in the shower.

Like at the other camps, the Japs would beat us prisoners at Zeblon Field. Even more disturbing at Zeblon Field, however, was the frequent beatings the men took for no apparent reason. Many of the men told me that the guards on the airfield detail were getting tougher and were striking the Americans regardless of the fact that the men were working hard. And on several occasions when the men complained about the rations I would later see them being beaten with rifle butts or clubs by six or seven guards. I think the reason for these beatings and treatment was because of the air raids that were being staged by American planes on the nearby islands about that time, and the Japanese guards were realizing that in the not too distant future American troops would be landing on the Island of Luzon where we were.

Again, there at Zeblon Field as at Nielsen Field, the guards would walk through the shacks at night and pick out a certain man saying that he didn't work hard enough that day and slug the hell out of him with either their fists or rifle butts, or both. I think this practice centered on several particularly mean, sadistic guards who had some special reason for punishing Americans; possibly as a means of exploiting their own superiority. During the night, if a man was seen by a guard taking a few puffs on a cigarette because he couldn't sleep or even while he went to the *benjo*, he would be escorted or dragged to the guard house where he'd be tortured. Usually, this torture took the form of having bamboo strips tied to the prisoner's arms and legs, and then leaving the prisoner tied this way in an awkward and uncomfortable position for the next several hours.

The men were losing weight at a rapid rate due to the unbalanced and insufficient diet. Everyone walked around the camp looking like skeletons. Damn near every man had ulcers on his legs and abrasions on his skin that became ugly, festered sores; there were no medicines to help. Some of the men walked, or rather limped, with bent over bodies and unsteady gaits. Still others would start breathing heavily just from walking. Several of the men, including me, experienced difficulty breathing from the pleurisy that had developed in the jungles of Palawan. This pleurisy resurfaced when working in the mud and water, even when working in the cookhouse; the coughing never stopped. All of these men, who were once physically able to endure almost any reasonable treatment, were now pitiful specimens ready to collapse. They were all, however, enduring the hard work and cruel treatment in an effort just to stay alive.

I well recall the night my buddies told me that one of the men was missing from a work detail. The next morning when the detail was marching to the airfield for work, the missing man's body was found full of bayonet holes. This was an inhumane act that could only be performed by a crazy maniac—a true indication of many of our Japanese guards.

As I stated before, at times the Japs would deliberately withhold water from American prisoners at some of the camps, sometimes shutting off the water faucet before everyone got their share of water. The guards at Zeblon Field were no different. We didn't care about water for bathing, because it would rain for about five minutes every afternoon. Our main concern was water for drinking; if we had to work, we had to drink. Many of the men were of the opinion that it was all dependent upon the temperament of our camp commander. This may have been true because officials higher up in rank may have chided the camp commander because the airfield wasn't yet ready for the defense of Manila in case of an American air raid. It always came back to the same method, the same idea the Japanese had of getting us to dig more dirt and rocks: *shigoto tocson, messy tocson* (work very much and you get much food).

At the beginning of 1944 I could tell that the Japs were worried because they started bringing newspapers with them to work in order to read the news. We always managed to get a copy of one of these and our interpreter would read it and tell us where the fighting was taking place. We would, however, form our own opinion about the wins and losses reported in the newspapers. We had good reason to believe that the Americans were advancing on all fronts because at night a great number of planes would fly over the Manila area, and during the day the Jap guards talked a lot about airplanes. We understood several Japanese terms and expressions relative to war and could understand that it wasn't Japanese airplanes the Jap guards were talking about. I could tell the guards were nervous, and told several of my buddies that we had to be careful not to give the more maniacal type of guards an opportunity to strike us because we figured they would soon be using their bayonets.

We worked steadily and didn't talk too much while we did it, but, nonetheless, the guards were still difficult to satisfy. It was obvious that the Japs wanted to finish this airstrip as soon as possible, and the guards' smiling faces—the few that had smiled at us—went away. The guards also stopped engaging in any conversations with us. The happy, carefree attitude that some of the non-sadistic guards had displayed also went away and more Japanese officers appeared on the scene. I began to get a gut feeling that the whole situation was going to change in the near future, and soon rumors began to fly that we were going to leave. The word was soon out that the Japs needed help at home because they were sending all of their men into the military, and we also new that the Japs wanted to prevent the Americans from freeing us.

Within a week or two these rumors proved to be true. The Japanese were going to move as many men as possible out of the Philippine Islands to Japan, where they intended to use all able bodied men in the Japanese coal mines, factories, and docks. We were soon trucked to Bilibid Prison where there were several thousand other prisoners being processed to be shipped to Japan. While at Bilibid I met many of my old 4th Marine Regiment buddies I had known in Shanghai who, while held captive, had been placed in different prison camps throughout the Island of Luzon.

The sight at Bilibid Prison was a hell of a thing to behold. Many of the men were missing legs or arms, cripples walked around aided only by the wooden sticks they used for canes, and others, being partially blind from powder burns suffered on Corregidor, had bandages over their eyes. Many of the missing limbs were the result of the fighting on Corregidor, while others were the result of accidents incurred while working on the many different POW details. There were also a large number of men there who had been injured by shrapnel while defending the fortifications of Forts Drum and Hughes and several of the other Navy detachments during the battles of Bataan and Corregidor. [Some of Ed's 1st Separate Marine Battalion Marines had been sent to these fortresses as beach defenders when the unit was sent to Corregidor.[30]]

Little did I know what lay ahead of me in Japan. I never dreamed that the next fifteen months would be so rough and cruel, the worst days of my entire life. Except for the my leg ordeal at Zeblon Field, nothing came close to what I would endure at the Omine Machi coal mine in regards to the long, hard hours of work while on a starvation diet with little or no drinking water. My toughest boxing matches could not compare with the work, the beatings, and the "Hot Box" that was to await me in Japan. How I managed to survive, I don't know.

7 Hell Ship - From the Philippines to Japan

We were marched from Bilibid Prison to the Manila docks where an old, rusty transport was tied. The dock was very crowded; besides about 1,800 of us prisoners, there were roughly 500 Japanese guards, numerous Filipino dockworkers, and a lot of other people that seemed to have just come out to watch. It was like a madhouse, especially with the guards being both in an angry mood and in a hurry.

After we reached the dock, the guards continued right on yelling their *speedo, speedo* and hurriedly prodded us up the gangplank and onto the transport with their bayonets. After reaching the top of the gangplank and the ship's deck we were herded down a ladder and into the hold. This took quite a bit of time with the guards crowding more and more of us into the hold, pushing and shoving the men as they went.

When there were about 700 of us in the hold I thought the Japs would finally stop sending more down the ladder. But they didn't. They kept yelling, "*Koodo, koodo,*" telling us in the hold to move back to make room for more prisoners. We thought, "Hell, they can't get any more in," but the guards continued to push and shove another 200 or so men down the ladder. Under normal circumstances they probably wouldn't be able to get more than 400 men in the hold, but because we didn't have anything much other than what we were wearing, they were able to crowd around 900 of us in. Hell, it was so crowded there wasn't enough space for all the men to sit down at the same time, resulting in some standing, some sitting, and some lying down on the steel deck, and steel is not a comfortable platform for resting. It was just too damn crowded and I instinctively knew there would certainly be problems when night came and everyone would want to lie down to sleep.

As soon as the last man climbed down the ladder the Japs closed the hatch, leaving us in pitch darkness. Fresh air could only come in through the opened hatch, and with the hatch closed it soon became as hot as hell inside our hold. Within an hour, perspiration was running down our backs and bellies as if it was rainwater, and, as I feared, men soon began arguing about space. Some blows were exchanged, but, like in the cattle cars we had ridden in on our way to Cabanatuan, there really wasn't enough room to get up a good swing. The men wanted fresh air and were griping and yelling for the Japs to open the damn door. The noise in the hold grew, and all of a sudden the hatch door opened. Six Jap guards stood in the hatchway and as they yelled, "*Koodo, koodo*," they pulled the slides back on their automatic rifles and aimed them directly at us. It was plain to all of us that the Japs were ready to fire, and the noisemakers quickly shut up. Once the noise settled down the Japs again closed the hatch. If the men hadn't quieted up when they did, I truly believe the Japs wouldn't have hesitated in shooting twenty-five or thirty of us, just that quick.

About an hour after the guards threatened us with their automatic rifles, they again opened the hatch. It was good to see daylight and sunshine once more. I can tell you that one quickly learns to appreciate fresh air after spending time in such a tight spot. Throughout our trip, for the most part, the Japs kept the hatch door open during the days, but closed it every evening as soon as it became dark outside, which made for some very long, hot, stuffy nights.

We more or less had to cooperate with each other in the hold, taking turns sitting, standing, and lying. Nevertheless, there were a few wise guys that wanted to be comfortable themselves without regards to the next man. This type of behavior led to arguments and name calling such as "You dirty bastard," "You damn fool," or "You son of a bitch." Many of the men being yelled at for causing the disturbances just laughed or cussed at the guys who did the yelling. We had to shut both of those kinds of men up for fear the Japs would open fire at us for making noise, and for our own sanity.

After about six or seven days en route, everyone was so damn hot, tired, and hungry that no one had any energy to waste on yelling at the man next to him, which took care of the arguments. Twice a day the Japs would lower three wooden buckets into the hold. Two contained rice and the third millet soup. Many of the times the rations weren't sufficient and a dozen or more men would miss a meal because the man serving the rations didn't give equal portions. While trapped in this hold, I soon learned things about a few individuals that I previously hadn't known. I previously didn't think people were so greedy and didn't give a damn about the next man's well being, knowing that the next man was just as hungry as they were.

We were also constantly thirsty, since our dear little friends didn't give us any water to drink during our voyage. I figured they thought the millet soup held enough water to take care of our thirst. My mouth, like everyone else's, soon became dry as hell and my lips were cracked and bleeding. Just one drink of cold water every day would have been refreshing. A cold bottle of beer wouldn't have been bad either; even Saki would have been ok.

The ulcers on our legs became troublesome, and with no medicine to heal the ulcers the flies kept settling on them. Besides the flies, large roaches were also crawling on us as well as upon the filthy steel deck, which was covered with urine and excreta. The Japs only sent down one bucket a day for all 900 of us to use as a *benjo*. One bucket for 900 men was hardly enough, and many of these men had diarrhea or dysentery and couldn't even wait for it to reach them. Many were the times when a man filled his pants; cleaning them was very difficult. We poor, suffering prisoners couldn't help ourselves, I included; the deck soon became a real mess.

Everyone was so hot and sweaty, and the stench was terrible, especially at night when the hatch door was closed and there wasn't any fresh air coming in. During the nights quite a number of men would pass out; they couldn't get out of the hold until morning when one or more were found dead, more or less from suffocation. A little cold water would have saved many of these men's lives. My mouth was so damn dry that I had no saliva.

All through the night you could hear someone complain, "Get the hell off my back," "Get your damn rear end out of my face," "Quit farting." Or "Move over you bastard or I'll kill you," "It's to damn hot with you so damn near," "I can't sleep with you bums talking all night." We just had to face it, it was hell and the Japs wouldn't help. It was especially difficult for men like me who had respiratory problems because it was very hard to breathe in the hot, smelling, stifling air. I always welcomed the morning when the hatch door was opened and the fresh air came in—what little actually did come in.

On one particular day two men began fighting in the hold, resulting in creating so much noise that the guards fired two shots in the air; the men quickly stopped their fight. Fighting in the hold was foolish for several reasons. First, because there was really no space to fight in—no space to stand up and swing at each other, and no space to wrestle. Second, because a man needed all his strength just to survive, and fighting just wasted his energy. And third, especially after this last incident, everyone knew that the Japs wouldn't hesitate to shoot in the event of any more fighting, or too much noise for that matter. Either way, after this last incident, I was quite positive there would be very few, if anymore arguments or fist-a-cuffs for the remainder of our trip.

It really did stink in the hold during the night because of all of the sweaty bodies and the gas released from the excreta. Most of the excreta was near the hold opening, because that's where the really sick men with diarrhea and dysentery usually stayed. They had to be boosted topside more often than the rest of us to be sprayed down with fire hoses in order to be cleaned off.

Many of the men wanted to lie or sit directly beneath the hatch door. The first few days of the trip I also stayed near the hatch opening. During the nighttime this spot was the best location, but during the day it was the worst. I found that it was very hot right under the opened hatch in the daytime with the sun burning down, and it was just too much for the body to endure for ten hours a day. I also realized that it was not only hot there, but there was also a lot of confusion there. Soup would spill over from time to time as it was lowered down, and on several occasions the Japs turned the fire hose directly down into the hold. If you were at the bottom of this opening, you received the brunt of both this spilled soup and the fire hose. In addition, men had to be lifted up and helped down the ladder, and the *benjo* buckets filled with urine and excreta were lowered and raised by a rope; several times these also spilled and fell on the men directly below the opening. And it was the men just below the hatch that the guards had threatened to shoot those times when there was too much noise in the hold.

The men that did stay there also sweated profusely and fell over like flies. When one of the men would faint, several of us would have to boost him up the ladder in order to get him topside were he could cool off for a while. The guards would hose these guys off with a fire hose and then send them back down again. I recall several times that men collapsed completely from heat stroke and required more than just a cooling off.

Therefore, I decided to make my way back towards the bulkhead where, although it was hot, the sunrays wouldn't be beating down on me all day long and I would be away from a lot of the confusion. It took about two days to inch my way back, because everyone thought that the spot they were in was the best in the hold and no one wanted to give theirs up. Many of the men would not move an inch until I told them that I didn't want their spot; that I was just moving to the bulkhead. Once I finally made it back there, I found there was sufficient space to lie down and rest, or just sit with my back leaning against the steal bulkhead.

I estimated that the temperature directly below the hatch opening was about 110 to 120 degrees, whereas the temperature by the bulkhead was only about 100 degrees. After the first few days, the men in the hold, especially those that were by the hatch opening, stood or laid about dopey and dizzy, to the extent that a lot of them didn't even know anymore where they were or what was happening. Several of them sat on one spot for days on end and didn't move six inches, while others would lie in one spot until someone kicked and pushed them aside; others appeared to just sleep for days. When I saw a man in bad shape due to malaria or overcome by heat, I would tell others to allow the man to have more space or let him get some fresh air.

Not only did I have more space to relax in the rear of the hold by the bulkhead, I also didn't have to listen to a lot of B.S. from the men next to me. This gave me the chance to quietly think to myself, and I began to wonder how long it would take to get to Japan. I figured it would probably take two, three, or even four times as long as a normal trip because there were American submarines patrolling the waters. The regular shipping routes would be watched by the subs, forcing our transport to take a zigzag course, lengthening our trip's distance and time.

The nights back by the bulkhead were also different than the nights I had spent by the hatch opening. Back there by the bulkhead I could very plainly hear the huge waves splashing against the side of the ship and the pounding of the ship's engines, which seemed to struggle harder when the sea was rough. I could hear the ship creak when the waves were triple their normal size during the storms we passed through, tossing the ship around. It rained all through many of the nights, and the thunder and lightning, coupled with the complete silence throughout the ship, with the exception of the sound of the engines, created a scary atmosphere during these dark nights. Every noise was very clear, and several times I thought the old transport might even split at the seams. But, evidentially, it had made these trips before and was still seaworthy.

It was pitch dark at night in the hold, and a feeling of uneasiness would come over me. I would also get an inner feeling that at any time an

American submarine might send a torpedo through the side of the ship; a man's chance of getting out of the hold was nil.

I still remember that I was very hot on the Hell Ship and had probably a hundred nightmares. Millions of things went through my mind back then, events that happened during my entire life. Events when I was a little boy in Maplewood, Wisconsin, working with my father in his blacksmith shop, events from my boxing and wrestling days in Wisconsin and Michigan, of riding the rails, and many of the other things I had done. It seemed that during those days and nights onboard that old transport I covered almost my entire life up until that time.

While onboard the ship, I found that when one is in a ticklish situation one begins to think about death. I pictured myself jumping overboard after the ship had been torpedoed by an American submarine and being shot at, along with my buddies, by Japanese machineguns as we tried to swim away. This thinking brought back memories of my stay in Cabanatuan, Bilibid Prison, Palawan, McKinley Field, Nielsen Field, and Zeblon Field, and the troubles I had at each of these places; the dysentery, the pleurisy, my smashed foot, the beatings. And I remembered my leg operation, and the fact that it could have gone either way.

To this very day I can still picture the nights when the transport's engines would stop. All the lights were out and there were no voices to be heard; many of the men were probably praying. This created an atmosphere of pure loneliness, even though there were 999 other men surrounding me. My heart would beat faster until the engines again started up.

I believe everyone had mixed reactions as to what he would do in the event of an emergency. It somehow seemed easier to accept anything that happened during the daylight hours than at night. I always thought that American pilots and sub captains would be able to identify the Japanese ships that were carrying prisoners. I was wrong. I later learned that the doctor that saved my leg at Zeblon Field went down when a torpedo launched from an American submarine hit the Japanese Hell Ship he was on. [In fact, the Japanese did not outwardly identify their ships that carried POWs, therefore, Allied sub commanders and pilots had no way of knowing if the ships they were attacking carried POWs. According to Japanese figures alone, twenty-three Japanese ships carrying Allied POWs were sunk either by torpedoes or bombs, killing 18,901 POWs; 36,378 other POWs made it safely to Japan.[31]]

I must have been in a daze and even unconscious for days while below deck on the *Noto Maru*, because I do not recall eating, drinking, or even speaking to anyone for about five to ten days. During this time I didn't know what the hell was going on, and probably didn't even give a damn whether or not I had anything to eat or drink. The other men probably thought that I must have been sleeping and figured they had best just leave me alone. I really didn't care what anyone did or didn't do during my journey onboard the *Noto Maru*; the only thing that mattered to me was that I made it all the way. [The *Noto Maru* was built by Mitsubishi and owned and operated by Nippon Yusen.[32]]

I believe we lost about a dozen men on our trip en route to Japan due to various causes, a few even might not have been able to take it any longer and just banged their head against the bulkhead until they died. The dead men were hoisted topside, wrapped in a few blankets, and slid overboard on a slide made of planks designed just for that purpose. There were no ceremonies, just a splash in the water, the bodies being swallowed up by the huge waves, becoming shark bait.

One clear day the ship stopped for several hours. I was really surprised to hear that we had stopped so the Japanese could take supplies to a leper colony. Honestly, I could hardly believe the Japs could display this act of mercy towards others, especially after the way they had treated us and since they were in such a hurry to get us to Japan.

Finally, after countless days and nights [according to Jeanette Babler, Don Vidal, who was also onboard the *Noto Maru* with Ed, stated that the trip took about eleven to twelve days], on a sunny morning the ship stopped and the guards opened the hatch doors and almost immediately began shouting their commands of *speedo, speedo* and *koodo, koodo* for us to hurry up and get out of the hold. [The *Noto Maru* is reported to have arrived in Moji Japan from Manila with 1,036 live American POWs[33] on 6 September 1944.[34]]

We slowly began to climb the ladders. None of us could move very fast because we were all sore and stiff from either lying in the same cramped position or trading off sitting and standing within the same few feet, sometimes inches, of space for the past several days. We were all happy to be getting out of the hot, smelly hold, and would be glad to breathe fresh air again. I didn't think I could make it out of the hold on my own accord, but two buddies helped by boosting me up the ladder. Meanwhile, the Jap guards, beginning to lose patience and wanting us to vacate the ship as soon as possible, started to use their rifle butts to hurry us along.

Some of the men were in worse shape than I was in, and, being considered basket cases, were removed with stretchers. What happened to these helpless and defenseless men I don't know for sure, but I imagine that the Japs just disposed of them.

As the rest of us staggered down the gangway we were sprayed with a powder form of disinfectant, so much so that my whole body was covered with the powder. I assumed that this was to kill any bugs or germs that we had come in contact with either before leaving Manila or aboard the ship while en route to Japan.

After everyone was offloaded from the transport, the guards separated us into two groups and had us sit in the hot sun. It took them several hours before they finally made up their minds as to which group would work on the docks and which group would work in the coalmines. Many of my buddies boarded a train headed to the docks at Yamagata, the rest of us, just before dusk, began marching into a mountainous are.

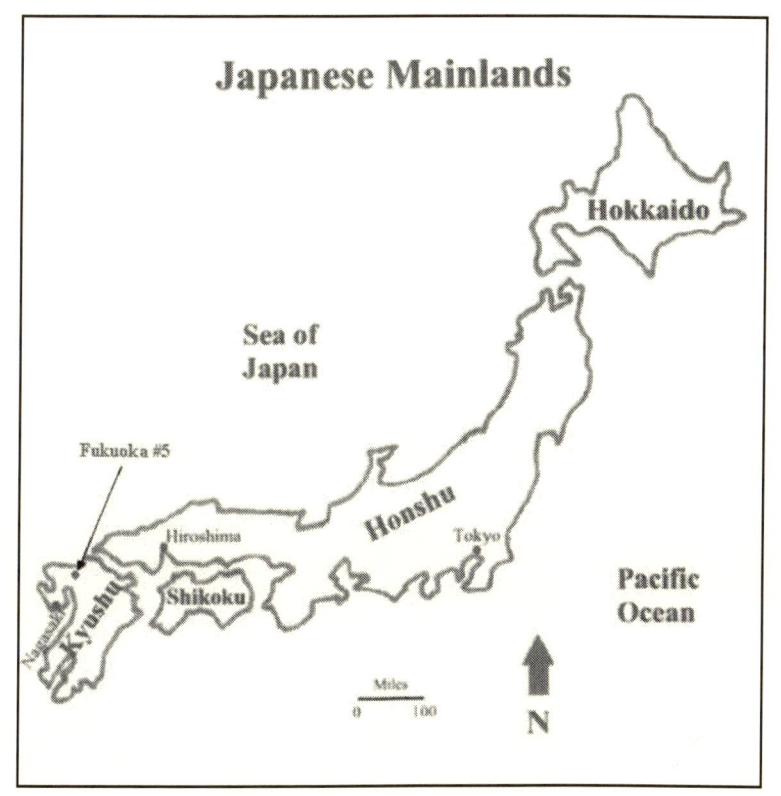

Map 4: Japanese Mainland

8   Mining Coal in Japan

It began to rain as we walked, and we were soon slipping on the muddy path, but the guards kept us moving with their ever constant *speedo, speedo*. I believe the guards were familiar with the road we were on, but it was all strange to us, and being pitch dark it was very difficult to keep up. Many of my buddies, still being weak and stiff from our long ride in the hold of the cramped transport, fell to the ground. We walked for hours this way, and when we finally reached the small mining town of Omine Machi we were all wet and muddy, but were also happy to be finally walking through the gates of our new camp, which was located adjacent to the town.

[Although Ed repeatedly refers to this camp as Omine Machi, the POW camp that he and his fellow POWs had just marched into was officially known as Fukuoka Camp 05B-Omine, or more simply Fukuoka #5, and was located on the southern Japanese Island of Kyushu. This seems to be a common area of confusion, even to the POWs who lived at the POW camps. The confusion comes from another POW camp on Honshu Island, Hiroshima #6 camp, which was in Omine-machi. Both of these camps were commonly called "Omine camp." A roster of the Fukuoka #5 camp lists Ed, as well as most of those he later mentions being in the Onime Machi camp, as actually being in the Fukuoka #5 camp. However, to better keep with Ed's original memoirs, the author has chosen to continue to use the name of Omine Machi, as Ed referred to the camp.[35]]

Almost immediately after entering the camp a guard took my dirty shorts, socks, and shoes, the same ragged, dirty clothes I wore for the past eighteen months, and discarded them to be burned. We were then marched to a bathhouse where we were allowed to bathe and relax in a cement tub filled with hot water. To my surprise, the guard at the bathtub even gave us a little extra time to relax in the hot water, which was really appreciated.

Soaking in the tub felt really good; especially after our chilly, wet walk through the mountainous area on the way to the camp. After the bath the guards gave us cotton underwear, a set of overalls, a jacket, and a pair of rubber mining shoes. Then each man was assigned a number, which we fastened to the left-side chest area of our jacket where it could be plainly seen at all times. This number was for identification; mine was *Shi Shichi Go*, which was Japanese for 475. From that point on I was referred to by that number. Every time we were assembled in camp we had to count off using our assigned number, and if I was wanted for something, a guard would say, "*Shi Shichi Go*, you come here."

After we received our clothes and numbers we received another surprise. We were marched to the dining hall, which was connected to the cook's shack, where we received a bowl of hot soup, rice, and hot tea. This really hit the spot. After finishing our meal we were assigned to an eighty-foot long by twelve-foot wide thin clapboard sided shack, which had windows on two sides. These windows slid open and were used as doors as well as by the guard patrol to observe our actions.

Each shack was divided into rooms that were eight-foot by eight-foot square; each of these rooms housed four men. Each man had his own mattress and blanket; another welcomed surprise. I believe the hard labor we would be doing in the coal mine was the reason for the mattresses; a man really had to get his rest to enable him to work hard the next day. Our eight-foot by eight-foot rooms were just large enough to accommodate the four mattresses, each touching the other, and an approximate three-foot shelf, which was located at the foot of the mattresses. These shelves were used to store our meager possessions: towel, soap, toothbrush, tooth powder, jacket, and pants.

Each room had a broom which we were to use to keep our straw-matted floor swept clean every day—the rooms were supposedly checked for cleanliness each day. On one side of the buildings was an overhang with a three-foot platform. This platform was used for our morning and evening *bango*. Including these two *bangos*, the Japs held about ten *bangos* each day at Omine Machi. We also left our rubber mining shoes on this covered platform. A strict rule, which we always had to adhere to, was that no one was allowed to walk on the straw mat that covered the floor of our rooms while we were wearing our rubber mining shoes. If we did, the mat would get dirty from the coal dust.

It was also a very serious offense to be late for a *bango*, especially the *bango* that was held prior to our leaving the camp for the mine, because being late for this *bango* would hold up the entire group. I quickly learned to be prompt for all formations because the guards didn't accept any excuses, and being late usually resulted in receiving three or four blows from a rifle butt along with a damn good scolding. These beatings and scoldings, however, depended on the particular sergeant of the guard on duty; some were stricter than others, with the stricter ones demanding punctuality at all times.

Although it was against the rules to enter our rooms while wearing our rubber mining shoes, if, just prior to *bango*, we forgot something in our room that we wanted to bring along with us to the mine, instead of taking the time to remove the shoes before entering our room, we would just tiptoe into the room and get the item. This was a better risk than risking receiving a beating for being late for *bango*.

At the front end of the shacks was a water tank, which had five faucets. This water was used for drinking, but not for washing, because, flowing down from the mountains, the water was ice cold. The water tank was my first stop during the summer months each day upon my return from the mine. In the winter months, however, it was too cold to drink.

The winter months of 1944-45 were cold as hell. I never saw a thermometer, but there was always an inch or two of snow on the ground, and it felt like it was always below zero. When we stepped out of our shacks in the morning the snow would crack and creak with our every step, and it was damn cold when walking down the road in the mornings on the way to the mine. During this mile and a half walk my whole body was cold. I kept my hands busy rubbing my ears, nose, and cheeks in attempts at keeping them warm. But regardless of these attempts, my ears were so cold they were nipped several times. I believe it is because of this that even today my ears can't take much cold air on them.

The area of Japan that we were in contained many coalmines, including the one we worked in, and there was probably a million tons of coal piled about a hundred feet high all over the area. I believe that we had a legitimate complaint because we were not allowed to use any of this coal to heat our shacks in the winter. I know the Japs could have used five or ten pounds of this coal every night in each one of our shacks without jeopardizing their own situation.

Although it was cold in the winter, during the summer months of 1945 it was hot as hell in our shacks, especially because we were not permitted to leave the windows open on both sides of our rooms at the same time. If we had been, we would have at least had a nice draft.

The camp itself was about four acres in size and consisted of a dozen shacks for the prisoners, a cook shack with a dining area, a supply building, and several shacks for the guards. It was surrounded by a heavy barbed wire, fifteen-foot high fence, which slanted inward at the top. My shack was about twenty-five feet away from this fence. On the other side of the fence was another fence made of wood. It prevented us from looking at the people in the city of Omine Machi, whose houses were only twenty or thirty feet on the other side of this later fence. The houses were close enough, however, that I could hear radios playing in them during the evenings. All around the inside of the compound next to the wire fence was a six-foot open area that none of the prisoners were allowed to step into. We could be expected to be shot if we did, and not doubting it, we stayed away from the fence area.

Guards were stationed in roof-covered shacks that were designed to protect the guards from the sun and the rain. These shacks were positioned at about sixty-foot intervals all along the barbed wire fence. In addition to these guard shacks, there was also a main guard shack located at the main gate entrance that was manned by an additional fifteen guards. Centered in this guard shack was a machinegun mounted on a tripod pointing directly at our shacks. The guards in all of these shacks were typical of the guards in the other camps that I had been in; sitting very erect on stools and armed with bayonet-fixed rifles. The guards also had a whistle, which they would use as an alarm. Other Jap guards patrolled the entire inside and outside perimeter of the compound. The main gate itself was reinforced with a heavy steel plate.

I didn't think any of us would ever attempt a breakout because it would have been foolhardy for an American or Englishman to attempt an escape in a country populated by 100 percent Japanese; there would be no place to hide. Besides, I believe that when at the camp in Japan we all had an optimistic outlook on the progress being made in the war, especially after reading reports in some Japanese newspapers that the war was being fought on their own home front.

When we first arrived at the camp, there was one eight-foot square concrete bathtub for 450 men to bathe in. The water in this tub was never changed until all 450 of us had bathed in it. If we didn't get into the tub with the first group we had no chance of getting clean because the water became too damn dirty. Therefore, as many men as possible would attempt to get into the tub in the first group when the water was still clean. Many times it was so crowded, especially in the first group, that we couldn't wash our own backs, so we ended up washing the guy's back in front of us while the guy behind us washed our back.

Somehow the English always made it in the tub before us Americans did because they returned from the mine earlier. There were 300 of us Americans to the approximate 150 English in the camp. The English also assumed that they had more to say about the camp procedures than we did because they had been living in the camp longer than we had; they were already there when we arrived from the Philippines. [In November 1942, 180 British prisoners became the first occupants of the Omine Machi coal mine POW camp.[36]] There were arguments about this. It appeared as though the English didn't care to associate with us and we felt the same way about them. In fact, their senior officer attempted to tell us about our rights, to which we soon informed him that we only took orders from the Japanese.

Arguments arose over the use of the bathtub; the English thinking they should use it first, making it impossible for us to get clean after they had had their baths. Our officers [Captain Jerome McDavitt (24th Field Artillery Philippine Scouts) was the senior American Commander at Omine Machi[37]] went to the Jap commandant and told him that we could not get clean with only one tub. For once our request didn't result in beatings, and the Japanese built an additional, larger eight-foot by twelve-foot tub for us Americans to use. After working in the mine for about twelve hours a day, we really appreciated the clean, hot water, and with the new tub there were no more arguments about who took the first bath.

There were huge bugs crawling around the place, especially in the summer time when it was hot. It seemed as though they came out of the straw mats. There were also little lizard-like vermin all over the place. During the winter months, however, these bugs and lizard creatures didn't bother us; but flea-type of creatures did. They liked to stick around in the blankets and mattresses where it was warm. The Japs didn't give us any repellent, saying that everything, including coal and insect repellent, had to go towards the war effort. So, with the mattresses so close together, when one man in a shack had bugs crawling around his mattress or blanket, it wasn't long before everyone else in that shack had these same bugs. I recall that during my stay at Omine Machi, on every one of my two to six nightly trips to the *benjo*, I would always see at least one of the men sitting up picking fleas off of his back.

Crabs hit a number of men also, including me. Since we didn't have any ointment for combating them, buddies would take turns shaving each other's entire bodies about every three days until the little pests disappeared. We had to have a lot of patience to help each other out of such a situation, and I can say that I had some real Marines with me during those months in Japan.

During the cold, damp fall and winter months a mattress and blanket were greatly appreciated, but during the summer months, because the guards wouldn't allow us to leave the glass doors open during the nights, it was hotter than hell in our rooms. The perspiration rolled off our bodies and ended up soaking our mattresses and blankets. In addition to smelling of my own sweat, my blanket was also rather dirty from the coal dust, and all the while I was in Japan it was never cleaned. Other than the bath upon returning from the mine each day and the removal of our rubber mining shoes before entering our rooms, there wasn't much difference in camp cleanliness at Omine Machi than there had been at any of the other camps I was in. We were given soap for bathing, but it wasn't any good, resulting in it being darn near impossible to keep our bodies as clean as they should be. And many times I wasn't able to wash my clothes for months on end because it would rain on the one day a month we had off, which was the only time available to wash our clothes.

One of the things I hated the most while I was in Japan was the early morning wake-up calls. At 3:30 a.m. a guard would come by the shack and hit each door four times with a club. It was so loud you couldn't miss the noise. We had to get right up and in seconds be dressed in our pants, shirt, socks, and rubber shoes. This was double tough during the winter because it was so damn cold.

The guards at Omine Machi were more particular than our previous Japanese guards regarding our replying to their questions, such as insisting that we reply with either "*hai*" or "*ni*," meaning yes or no. Their favorite expression, however, was the same as that of the Japanese guards in the Philippines, "*Speedo, speedo, shigoto tocson*," faster, faster, work very hard. [Many of the guards in the Japanese main islands, such as those guarding Ed, were not military but employees of large Japanese companies, such as the one that owned the coal mine Ed and his fellow prisoners were mining. These companies also provided what little housing, food, and clothing the prisoners where given. The Omine Machi mine was owned and operated by Furukawa Mining.[38]]

Our daily schedule was tight at Omine Machi. For an example, every day while on the day shift—each month we would change shifts from day to night—we were up at 3:30 a.m. and were expected to be dressed and at the dining hall in fifteen minutes. As we passed the cook in the dining hall he would give us our ration of *lugao*, the same type of watery rice we had had since our capture, which, as always, was in too small amounts. Another cook would hand us a soybean bun about the size of an American hamburger bun. However, unlike a hamburger bun, this soybean bun was hard. It was intended that we carry it with us to the mine as our noon meal.

Many of the men were so hungry, however, that they would just eat the bun right then as part of their breakfast; others waited until we reached the mine shack and toasted the bun over the potbellied stove located there. Still others kept their soybean bun in their pocket, eating it during their ten-minute lunchtime break as intended. A few, however, would trade theirs, probably because, although edible, the buns were made of bean flour and were hard and had no distinctive taste. But by that time we were so damn hungry that very few of us wouldn't nearly always eat everything we were given, regardless of the taste, even dog meat on occasions. And although the bun didn't taste very delicious, it was something to eat.

After our breakfast we would line up for a *bango* prior to marching to the mine. On our first day of work at Omine Machi we were again instructed on the Japanese method of counting. We started off on the wrong foot that first day, because, while lining up in front of the guard shack we fouled up our first count and, by the time the second count went wrong, the sergeant of the guard was quite disgusted and angry with us. He scolded us for about a minute in his native Nippon and then proceeded to punish the two men that caused the foul up. The third count proceeded to go ok. In the winter months we especially didn't like to foul up the count, because regardless of how cold it was, we would stand all lined up shivering until the count was finally correct.

We then marched in columns of four to the mine. During the winter months the guards would sometimes allow us to trot to the mine because they too were cold, although they had earflaps, gloves, and warm clothes; none of which we had. Nor did we have anything to cover our faces from the cold, not even a handkerchief, which made it rough—and it was cold; I mean cold! Quite a large number of men froze parts of their faces on these cold mornings.

Our noses would be running like hell, which, without handkerchiefs, we had to wipe on our jacket sleeves. On one cold morning after we had

Robert C. Daniels

reached the mine shack and as we were lined up for another *bango*, my nose was really running like hell and I wiped it on my jacket sleeve. A very small Jap guard, wearing white gloves, quickly came over to me and slapped me across the face. Then, after the count was ok, this same guard came to me and said, "*Shi Shichi Go*, you come here." When we reached the rear of the building, five guards wearing leather gloves took turns punching me. Just to make them think they were really hurting me, I made it a point to hit the ground about five times while they were slugging me. After about five minutes of this, they finally quit beating on me; I think they just got tired.

Quite a number of times the day crew would pass the night crew going too or coming from the mine. We never spoke to the other crew because it was too hot in the summer and too cold in the winter. Besides, the guards wouldn't allow us to speak anyway, not even to members of our own crew, at least not unless we were waiting in the mine shack for the other crew to come out of the mine. The first shift, the day crew, was awakened at 3:30 a.m. and returned to the camp at around 5 p.m. The second shift, the night crew, worked all night, returning to the camp at about 4:30 a.m.

We had all been issued miners caps, which had lights fastened to them. Once we arrived at the mine we would wait for about fifteen minutes for the previous shift to come out of the mine and then we'd board the mine train for the ride down to the 1st level. Our job was two more levels down from there; it took us about twenty-five minutes to walk those last two levels. The only lighting available was the lights on our miner's caps and a few small 25- or 30-watt bulbs, which were only placed about every seventy-five or eighty feet. All the while we walked the guards would be hollering their usual *speedo, speedo*.

I believe that just about every mine has water in it, and this one was no different. Everyday inside the mine I would step in water; this ensured that my feet were constantly wet throughout the day's work. Besides the water being bothersome, the mine was constructed to accommodate the shorter Japanese, not someone like me at six feet tall. As a result, I always had to walk slightly bent over whenever I was in the mine. Whenever I would straighten up my head would hit the supporting timbers. I ended up hitting my head on these beams an average of six times a day. Doing the math, this adds up to about 2,700 times, which eventually had quite an effect on my balance. For several years afterward I would fall down while working. I once even broke a couple of ribs while bathing. I also skinned my shins roughly twenty-five times, had dizzy spells, blurred vision, and even four car accidents, all as a result of my having continuously hit my head in the mine. This, plus the wet conditions I worked under may very well be responsible for the spinal arthritis I suffer with even today.

After we reached the job site in the mine we began picking and shoveling coal from up in a drift, which was a six- or so foot wide, thirty-five degree angled horizontal opening about five to six feet opposite and above the rail tracks. A steel chute was extended from the tracks to the end of the drift. A guard would send two men up the drift with scoop shovels and picks. It was the job of these two men to pick the coal loose and shovel it down the chute until the coal car was loaded. These same two prisoners would then push the coal car about 100 feet down the tracks to where the Japs would attach a cable and pull it to the next level, and from there on out of the mine.

A guard always stood below the drifts on the rails, and if the coal did not come down fast enough he would pound on the chute indicating that the two men up in the drift needed to work faster. If the two prisoners did not soon respond with more coal, the guard would start climbing up the drift hollering the all too familiar *speedo, speedo, shigoto tocson*. And he wouldn't hesitate to use his rifle butt or a club to speed up the workers. The drifts were always so dusty and dirty from the coal dust they contained that you couldn't see your partner. As a result, we ended up breathing in all of this dust and dirt and were spitting coal dust all the while we were at Omine Machi.

We really had some rough and tough guards on our detail, always pushing for more work and not easing up until the workday ended. If we saw a light coming up the drift we knew we had better work faster or we'd suffer the consequences of being beaten. There were very few days in the mine that I wasn't slapped, hit with fists or the butt of a rifle, or felt the point of a bayonet; and there was never a valid reason for this. It didn't matter how hard I worked each day, I'd still receive some sort of punishment by the guards. They would just start hollering, "*Koodo, koodo, speedo, speedo,*" and then systematically begin to beat on me. I remember hundreds of times looking back while pushing the loaded coal cars down the track always to see a guard following me with his bayonet-fixed rifle, and he never wore a smile. The guards also seemed to love showing off their authority, usually by very loudly shouting out their commands. It seemed as if they were trying to out do one another in this.

I believe the Japanese guards enjoyed punishing us Americans because they truly thought they were a superior race. But, for the most part, I think they actually weren't very well educated. And I still think it just made those little five-foot to five-foot six inch men feel good to hit a big six-foot tall American. I honestly believe these little men figured that if they would keep hitting me then the big man would eventually fall over. They probably told their buddies and families how good it felt.

Pushing the coal cars was the part of the job that really used up our strength. We had to strain as we pushed the cars, and still the damn guards would be right behind us urging us with their rifle butts or bayonets every time we slowed down even a bit. These were the times I really had to control my temper, being tempted many of these times to turn around and kill the bastards.

Each day during my walk to the mine I would say a prayer, "Bless me, St. Joseph, that today I will have a successful day in the mine and that I will make it back topside. Watch me so I will not get hurt, or get angry and hit a guard, especially when he is following me while I am using all my strength pushing coal cars down the tracks."

Regardless of the fact that we worked our butts off, the sergeant would always try to increase the day's quota of cars loaded. The quota increase worked for a few days, but then it just became impossible for us to increase it any more. We were just not physically equipped to work any harder. This poor physical condition caused us to end up slowing each operation just a little bit, which caused the Japanese foreman to realize we were doing as much work as we were capable of, especially since we weren't eating steak every day. I know that if the pace had continued, as the Japanese had wanted it to, only a small number of us would have survived. Seven out of ten would probably have died. Even at the pace we were working, I was lucky to have made it.

Every day I would hear the loud noise of blasting coming from other parts of the mine. Although the mine itself must have covered many square miles, the blasting was often relatively close to where we were working. I was told that the blasting was intended to loosen the rock that needed to be removed before the coal was available for mining. The Japanese did all of the blasting; no doubt because they didn't want us to have access to the dynamite, which I couldn't blame them.

A Japanese mine foreman told me that the mines were originally constructed with the guidance of American engineers, so I figured that the mine was probably quite safe. All the same, when the blasting was close to us, dust would cover the area where we were working and I worried just a bit because the powerful explosions would sometimes temporarily block the mine with fallen debris. At times, as we walked out of the mine after our shift was over, we would come across the remnants of this fallen debris. I really never worried a hell of a lot though, because I knew I was being watched over by my guardian angel—I prayed so much every day that I must surely have received some help to survive all the punishment that I had received.

About 11 a.m. or so each day a guard would holler, "*Yasmay*," which meant rest, and we would sit down for ten minutes to eat our soybean bun; at least those who had actually saved their bun for lunch would eat them, the remainder would just rest. After the ten-minute break we would immediately go back to work picking and shoveling coal and pushing the cars down the track. This would go on non-stop until about 4:15 p.m. when we would begin our walk to topside.

Negotiating the first two levels of the mine was not too difficult, but the walk up the last level with its quarter mile length of thirty-degree grade was hard; the last 100 feet of which was always the hardest. Many of the men, including myself, fell repeatedly during these last 100 feet and had to somehow pick ourselves up and keep going; but, with a little more effort, we were always able to make it.

After we reached topside at about 5 p.m. we were counted once again to make sure no one had stayed in the mine. We then were marched back to the camp, which we reached at about 5:30 p.m. Once back inside the camp we were assembled in front of the guard shack where we had another *bango*. After this count was ok, we made a dash towards the bathhouse; everyone wanting to get in before the water became too dirty. After our baths we would go to our shack to wait for dinner call.

I recall that many days in the spring and fall, the raining season when it would rain for two or three straight days, we were soaked by the time we got back from the mine. This left us cold and damp, and after *bango* a lot of these times we just ran to our shacks and climbed under our blankets where we shivered for about twenty minutes before taking our baths and waiting for dinner.

The dinners consisted of two bowls of millet soup, a small ration of rice, and a cup of very strong black tea. I think it was the hard work that we were doing in the mine that entitled us to the two bowls of soup. The soup, however, as it was in the Philippines, was inedible many of the times because of the hard vegetable stalks it contained. It sometimes even had the tendency of making me gag and heave. I realized, however, that I would have to eat whatever was offered to me in an effort to stay alive, and I usually saved my soybean bun, broke it into small pieces, and put it into my millet soup, allowing me to be able to better enjoy both.

On one of these days that I had decided to save my bun, I hid it well inside my mattress before I left for the mine, planning on mixing it with my soup that evening. I spent that day thinking about how much I was going to enjoy my dinner that night. As soon as the *bango* was ok after returning to camp that evening, I quickly ran into my shack and looked in my mattress. Sure as hell, some dirty bastard had stolen my bun! I was so damn mad I darn near blew my top and truly believe I would have killed the thief if I had found him. I went through every shack that night in an attempt to see who had stayed in camp that day, but I failed to find the man who stooped so low as to steal from his fellow American prisoner. It was probably just as well, because I do really believe I would have killed him, and not thought it wrong. Food was the main issue in my life at that time. If I hadn't needed every ounce of food I could get at the time I wouldn't have cared so much; I was always hungry and very weak.

By that time we had no energy left, and nearly every man in camp would go lie down on his mattress to rest after the evening meal. I would be so damn tired I would never even walk ten feet down the hall to visit with any of the men; no one was in the mood to talk anyway. We didn't have the stamina to continue the hard labor on the diet that we were living on, and we were all losing weight and strength on a daily basis.

In reality, we were not permitted to go to bed until after the nightly *bango*, which was at 8 p.m., and if you were not up and out on the platform a guard would come into your room with his rifle and hit you several times with it. We would, however, try to warn each other when the guards came by while one of us tried to get a little extra sleep.

My thoughts regarding the actions of the Japanese guards were that they were a collection of murderers who thoroughly enjoyed beating the American prisoners, especially me, a big 4th Marine who had come from Shanghai. Our guards at Omine Machi were quite aware of the 4th Marine Regiment's presence in Shanghai prior to the war.

I was told that the Japanese had a tradition in beatings, and we noticed that the Japanese officers would even punish their subordinates with beatings in our presence. The officers would knock them down and whack them with the flat of a saber. In turn, the Japanese non-coms [non-commissioned officers: sergeants and corporals] would beat the privates, the three star privates would beat the two star privates, and the two star privates would beat the one star privates.

Numerous incidents occurred at Omine Machi where I had to refrain from striking back at the guards, both at the camp and in the mine. Many of these times it became awfully hard to resist the temptation, but I had to maintain complete control of my temper in order to survive. Some of the men who knew me from my Shanghai days knew that I had done a considerable amount of boxing before the war. And several of the times when the Japs were beating on me some of these men would urge me on yelling, "Come on Ed," thinking I might actually take a swing at the guards. But I didn't want to take a chance.

In contrast, however, it seemed that when the Japanese guards were alone they were actually less belligerent, being bolder when other guards were near. An interesting example of this occurred to me one day while working in the mine. On this day one of the guards assigned me to the wrong work detail. I worked on the job all day, and at about 4:30 p.m. a different guard hollered, "*Shi Shichi Go*, you come here." After I walked up to him and the two of us were alone, the guard hollered, "*Kiotski*." I stood at attention and the guard started cussing at me in Japanese, evidently because I had been working on the wrong job throughout the entire day. He then took a wild swing at me with his rifle butt in an attempt to hit me on the head. I raised my right arm, pushed his rifle away, readied myself to exchange blows, and yelled, "Come on you yellow bastard."

To my surprise, the guard backed down and quietly took me back to the group that I had been working with. Not another word was said about the incident and I soon realized the guard had lost face. I had called his challenge and he was ashamed to mention anything to his co-workers. I would not have resisted the guard's attack on me if we had not been alone. Either way, though, if the guard had not backed down, I am quite positive that I would have tried to kill him. And I believe the odds would have been in my favor, because, even though as weak as I was, I had the greater incentive.

Another incident that I will never forget was the day when a guard told me to operate an eighty-pound pneumatic drill. He indicated that I should use it to loosen the coal up in a drift. I hesitated for a few minutes and tried to indicate that I couldn't do the job. The guard just went into a rage and began shouting, "*Koodo, koodo, speedo, speedo*," meaning, "Damn it, get moving and do it in a hurry." He then approached me holding his bayonet-fixed rifle in the guard position, so I decided I had better give it a try. I grabbed the drill, slowly raised it over my head, staggered, and fell, dropping the drill.

This time, as the guard shouted his *koodo, koodo*, he rushed towards me and hit me three times with the butt of his rifle. He then hollered, "*Baka, baka, speedo*," meaning, "Idiot, hurry up." I realized I had to definitely convince this guy that I truly was unable to handle the drill, and to do so I knew I had to put on a good act. So, with great effort, I raised the drill over my head, staggered some, pressed the on button for about four seconds, and then fell backwards, allowing the drill to fall on my chest. This maneuver finally convinced the guard that I could not effectively handle the drill and he threw up his arms in disgust, shouted, "*Koodo, koodo*," and motioned for me to get back on the job pushing the coal cars.

9 Surviving in Japan

At first, while at Omine Machi, I had seemed to be getting along quite well in the mine. Then the Japs made me work with an American who was on very friendly terms with them, to the point where he was shown special favors at my expense. He could speak Japanese and had told the Japs that he was married to a Japanese girl and had two little daughters by her. He was lazy and would talk and laugh together with the Japs, who were easy on him. While pushing the cars full of coal, this guy would attempt to make me think he was pushing as hard as I was by making a few grunts and groans, but as far as I was concerned he was a faker. I had pushed so many coal cars by this time that I could tell when my partner wasn't helping, and when this guy was teamed with me I could easily tell that he wasn't doing his share by how difficult it was for me to push the cars. He would say, "Come on Ed, push," when all the while the damn fool knew I was straining.

In the mine my little friends would make the initial opening for the drift, which satisfied their short, physical need, but it was too damn low for me. This poor excuse for a partner of mine should have been sent up in the drift to work because he was only about five-foot seven inches in height. It would have been much easier for him in such a cramped space than it was for my larger frame, but he would never have to climb up in the drift to pick the coal loose or shovel it into the chute. I, on the other hand, because of my size, had to pick and shovel the coal on my knees while up in the drift. After about three hours of this work, I was exhausted and my back ached, but I had to keep working. I thought about slugging this guy, but thought better of it because I knew he would turn me over to the Japs, who would then certainly take his side.

While in the Philippines this same guy was known to turn in fellow prisoners to the Japs if and when he had a losing fight with the other prisoners. I heard that while we were at Zeblon Field he turned another American over to the Japanese, and the next day the man that he turned over was found bayoneted to death. To think that a fellow American prisoner would turn another American prisoner over to the Japs was cowardly, disgusting, and unmerciful. There were also many times at the Omine Machi camp that this guy didn't have to work, but when he did he always told the Jap guards he wanted to push coal cars with me.

It was very difficult for me to work with him. My having to do so almost meant my complete downfall, because I rapidly lost weight and got weaker every day. After many days of pushing the loaded coal cars down the track with this Jap lover, I damn near fell over from exhaustion.

After working all day pushing the heavy coal cars with my bad partner I was ready for a break and welcomed the 4:45 p.m. quitting time, but I still had the long walk up the two levels, and many were the days I was lucky to make it back up to the first level.

After the war he was court-martialed and had been sentenced to ten months imprisonment, reduced in rank, and was ordered dishonorably discharged. The last I had read about his case it stated that the Supreme Court agreed to review his Navy court-martial conviction concerning charges against him; charges of striking two fellow prisoners while in Japanese prison camps. I never did read about the final result of his case, although I wish I had been called to testify. I believe I had a legitimate complaint, though I realize certain acts are hard to prove. [This may be Petty Officer Second Class Harold E. Hirshberg, USN, who was tried for treasonous activities after the war.[39]]

At about the five month time period of being at the Omine Machi camp, working the long hours in the mine really began to show on us. I was always really hungry, and by this time didn't have any reserve strength left. In addition, my body was slightly bent over because of the hundreds of times my head had struck the overhead timbers of the mine. My group at the time was working the night shift, and we would leave the mine soaking wet in the cold early morning air, returning to the camp about 4 a.m. while it was still dark outside. Working in the wet mine was not at all beneficial to my chest condition—I hadn't really completely recovered from the pleurisy I had suffered from in Palawan—and, although I didn't realize it at the time, I never stopped coughing all the while I was at the camp. Looking back at it, it's very surprising to me that we didn't lose more men to pneumonia with those cold, wet conditions.

Upon returning to the camp on those mornings, I would quickly walk over to the cook shack as soon as we were dismissed from *bango* and with my hands scrape the bottom of the rice pots hopeful that I might find some hard rice crust, even if it was only a few crumbs. I was continually looking for extra food, and being so damn hungry at the time if I didn't find any crumbs in the bottom of those pots I would literally go stand alongside my shack and cry. All the while we were so hungry the Japs had onions and cabbages growing throughout the compound just six or so feet from our shacks. I watched these onions and cabbages grow for weeks, and it wasn't long before they were ready to eat. The problem was that the guard shack was situated only about forty feet from my shack and the guards were always on the lookout for thieves, so attempting to steal the onions and cabbages was always a risky business.

However, once the onions and cabbages ripened I was able to manage to get a few after dark without too much trouble while I was on the day shift. During the daylight hours, however, the stealing was more difficult because it was light out and there seemed to be more guards on duty. But we did it anyhow, and although I never did like raw onions, they sure did taste good when I was that hungry, and they helped fill the empty spot in my stomach.

We would keep the guards' attention on one side of the building while stealing some of the onions and cabbages on the other side. We didn't dare to do this too regularly, however, or the guards would notice the empty spots. Onions we could take without being too easily noticed if we didn't take too many at one time from any one spot, but the cabbage was a different matter; they left a noticeably open space. Therefore, we had to take the cabbages from different areas in the compound each time. Nonetheless, since I had always liked cabbage as a kid back home in Wisconsin, I would rather risk my life stealing them than the onions.

It became quite apparent that we were becoming weaker and weaker with each passing day, because each day it became more difficult to perform our jobs in the mine. But the Japanese still did not improve our rations, and, not surprisingly, stating their usual, "*Speedo, speedo, shigoto tocson, messy tocson,*" the guards tried the same gimmick that was used on us in the Philippines, telling us that if we worked faster and harder we would receive more food, trying to get us to push more coal cars each day than what we had the day before. But after trying this again and again they finally gave up, realizing that a man could do just so much work and no more when he was tired, weak, and hungry. Even so, here in Japan the pressure was greater than it was in the Philippines; the Japs really needed the coal for their ships and factories.

During the winter months of 1944 it was so cold, especially since we didn't have any fires in our shacks to help keep us warm, that we would spend our time, when not at work in the mine, crawled under our blankets just to stay warm. During the winter of 1944 and the spring and summer of 1945 I believe we lost about twenty-two men due to starvation, extra hard labor, and pneumonia. In addition, several of the men just couldn't take it and cracked up mentally.

The human body can stand more than one would think, but in trying to survive under these abnormal conditions it just became a matter of time. I honestly believe that if we would have spent another winter at Omine Machi less than fifty of us would have survived. Because of the methods of treatment inflicted upon us, such as deliberately withholding food, water, and medicine, plus the hard slave labor, I would have to say that the Japanese were guilty of murder, because with just a minimum effort the Japs could have saved many of the POW's lives.

News was not easy to obtain in Japan because the Japanese were losing the war and they probably didn't want us to know all the details. However, around the period of the ending of hostilities there was an older Japanese man who watched us during the day as we worked. He would always bring in a newspaper and read it. When he was done with it, he would slip it into a crevice along side the tracks in the mine. Just before quitting time I would grab the paper as I pushed my last coal car of the day. We had two men in the camp that could interpret Japanese, and the next day they would give us a report on how the war was progressing. Three-fourths of the news stories were written in the Japanese favor—no doubt these were lies printed to lead the Japanese public into thinking Japan was winning the war—so we never believed everything we read, although it did give us an idea of where the war was being waged. For an example, if the paper said that an air battle over Honshu resulted in the Japanese knocking down twenty-five American planes while the Japanese lost two of their own, we just didn't believe the part about the plane losses. But we were happy to know that our forces were fighting in the many Pacific islands and the skies over Japan, and we knew that it would only be a matter of time before we would be free again.

Rumors always abounded throughout the POW camps; some turned out to be true, others were false. One rumor that circulated before 1945 had it that Japanese General Hideki Tojo was going to visit the Philippines—he never did. Another rumor had it that many of the Japanese Generals and members of the Japanese High Command had arrived at the conclusion that the American services (Marines, Navy, Army, and Coast Guard) were too powerful to be stopped by the Japanese, this, because our forces were taking over all the strategic Pacific islands, which would eventually lead to Japan's defeat. We also heard that high ranking officers of the Japanese Army and Navy were being relieved of their commands because their losses were so great.

It was about this time that we first saw American planes flying over the Island of Honshu. I believe the Japanese leaders realized that they were beginning to lose the ground war. Flights of United States Air Force [Army Air Corps] bombers were directed towards the larger Japanese cities, and every night we could hear them fly over and bomb their targets. We would open our doors to watch and listen; it was a beautiful sight to see and hear our own planes destroying the Japanese cities.

It was also about this time that the guards in our camp began changing their attitudes. I noticed their tempers were becoming very short and any violation of the rules by a prisoner began meaning harsher treatment. This I was to witness first hand a little later.

Although the attitude of the guards so abruptly changed, I began feeling better about the whole situation with the American planes flying over during their bombing missions. I recall that although walking up the grade of the mine to topside was so difficult, my whole body was suddenly filled with enthusiasm, and I was able to struggle just that much harder because I realized I was going to make it home. There was that extra feeling that soon we may not have to make too many more trips to the mine, and as I staggered and fell it became easier to pull myself up, regardless of how many times I would fall on the tracks. It appeared as though I had a renewed strength, somewhat like the old football phrase, "Run for Daylight."

In reality, though, it appeared as though in the spring of 1945 many of us had diarrhea so bad that someone was always gong to the *benjo*. I don't know whether it was the result of the dysentery we had had in the Philippines, but it was run, run, run all day and night. This itself left a man in a weakened condition, making it even more difficult to perform the hard labor still constantly demanded of us.

To add to this we spent about four months on a bean diet. The Japanese

Robert C. Daniels

must have confiscated a farmer's bean crop, and these beans tended to just pass right through my system whole, doing me little or no good. The millet soup they served us at that time was mixed with these same beans as well. The effect on my system was quite noticeable in the form of my bowel movements, which became very regular in that they occurred four, five, or six times each day.

Not once during this time did I ever sleep an entire night without having to run to the *benjo*. And I wasn't alone in this. At nearly any given time during a night there would be someone from our shack making a trip to the toilet. Our diarrhea problem didn't stop just because we went into the mine, either. The guards were apparently very aware of our condition, because whenever I would walk up to a guard in the mine and say, "*Benjo*," he would always say, "Ok," with hardly any hesitation. The bad part was that there wasn't a toilet in the mine. We would have to walk or climb up and do our business in an unused drift. The stench became quite bad in many of the places. There were also many times when a man wouldn't make it up into a drift in time and ended up filling his pants. He would then have to work for the rest of the day in his own filth. Later that night, after everyone had taken their bath, he would have to clean his pants out. And with only having the one pair of pants to wear as we did, it was difficult to dry them before having to leave camp for the mine the next day.

One day my Marine buddies told me that I was walking like a mechanical toy. They said, "Ed, you are pale, weak, and bony, and if you do not get out of the mine for awhile you will not go home with us." Prior to this, I had, for the most part, been oblivious to my condition. I knew that I had lost a lot of weight, but I didn't realize how weak of a condition I was actually in. It appeared that my strength had failed quite rapidly, and there had to have been a reason for it. Looking back, I am positive that the extra effort that I had to put forth pushing the coal cars working with that Jap lover drained my body of any extra energy I may have had. I wasn't the only man in this condition, however.

By this time we had all been together for several years and had all deteriorated physically at about the same rate. This deterioration seemed so gradual and we were so used to it that at first we hadn't really noticed just how drastic our physical conditions had changed. However, all of us by this time had become extremely thin and bony. Each of us looked to be in quite the same poor physical shape, without a fat or muscular man in the entire group. Our condition was more clearly noticeable while we were in the bathtub, because it was then that we could better see our bony bodies, covered only with shriveled skin. After we washed off the coal dust and dirt we looked like skeletons. Everyone's ribs and hipbones were protruding, and our shinbones and backbones stood out clearly. Our arms looked like broomsticks, our faces were thin and gaunt, and our eyes appeared to be set deep in our heads. The average weight of the men at the camp at Omine Machi was no more that 100 to 115 pounds.

About June of 1945—here I am only guessing the actual month, but the days were warmer and we saw the sun more often—my condition was apparently getting worse, and the Marines in the room next to mine told me that I should visit our camp's American Army doctor. The winter had been rough on me due to the combination of the pleurisy I had previously acquired on Palawan, the constant wet feet I had from working in the water in the mine, and the ever-present hunger and grueling slave labor. A few of my buddies were also having the same type of trouble. The long hours of hard labor and poor diet was affecting everyone. It became difficult to maintain our balances with our weakened legs, and tempers were very short, which soon caused a lot of arguments. So, in this condition, after work the next day, I went over to see the doctor, who was seated at a small table.

Upon my reaching the table the doctor look up at me and said, "What is wrong with you?" Standing there staggering and swaying I told him that I needed a few days rest in order to pull myself through. Although he could see the shape I was in, he just looked at me and said, "Why, you are one of the healthiest men in the camp. Go back to work."

I was mad, really mad. Mad as hell! If I hadn't been so weak I would have grabbed him and tried to kill him. But, even if I had been able to, I know the Jap guards would have done me in, so I wouldn't have won anyway. I ended up calling him a damn horse doctor, asking him where in the hell he had gotten his license to practice medicine from, and walked back to my shack. Once there I fell down on my mattress to rest. I was still really mad at the doctor, and while lying there on my mattress I seriously thought about going back and killing the dirty bastard. A short time later my buddies came in to see how I had made out—they too were really hot when I told them what had happened.

I honestly think the doctor favored the Army personnel, because I couldn't understand how in the hell he could deny me the privilege of working inside the camp for a few days in order to pick up a little energy and breathe some fresh air. Nonetheless, the next morning I went back to work in the hole.

I must really have looked rather bad off because I heard that my buddies had held a meeting and decided to speak to the doctor that had turned me down. I believe the Marines really told him off and probably even threatened him because one day soon thereafter the doctor came to me and informed me that I should stay in the camp the next day. This time when he spoke to me he was very polite and said that I should work around the camp, and that a guard would assign me a job to do the next day. Besides getting out of working at the mine for a few days, this also meant that I didn't have to push the coal cars with my Jap loving partner.

On my first day of work in the camp a guard gave me a pole and two buckets, along with a dipper, and told me to clean out all of the camp latrines. I filled the two buckets, placed one on each end of the pole, and then placed the pole on my right shoulder. Carrying the buckets this way I would dump their contents into a large hole about a hundred feet away. I looked just like the coolies had looked when they carried their bags and baskets back in Shanghai.

I had to put up with the stink, but it was a great relief to stay out of the mine for the six or seven days that I was allowed to stay in camp, and it probably saved my life. What helped me make it through all of this was realizing that one's mind has a lot to do with one's desire to live. With this in mind, I made it a point not feel too sorry for myself, believing that if I did I wouldn't make it back home.

I am grateful to all of the Marines at Omine Machi and sorry I didn't get a chance to thank each one personally. I hope those that I have not seen since our stay at the mine camp are able to read this and know that I do very much appreciate what they did to help me survive. The following is a list of those Marines that I would like to thank that worked with and helped me at Omine Machi. Included is the number I remembered they were assigned by the Japanese.

#458 Amerant, Raymond J.	#486 Hamby, Thornton E.
#459 Baker, Roger D.	#487 Hathorne, Walter W.
#470 Duncan, Louis E.	#488 LaFleur, George N.
#471 Pitzel, Daniel J.	#489 Hesler, James C.
#472 Turner, Gerald A.	#490 Lang, William J.
#473 Mc Clung, William J.	#491 Latham. John D.
#474 Richter, Adolph	#492 Lee, Charles R.
#476 Meyers, Malvern R.	#493 Matheny, Wilfred R.

#477 Russell, William G.
#478 Smith, Raymond E.
#479 Strickland, Eldon K.
#480 Vinson, Benjamin H.
#481 Fischer, Culver L.
#482 Graigg, Thomas R.
#483 Etter, Frank G.
#484 Fisher, George N. Jr.
#485 Gilbertson, Homer A.

#494 Ruzek, Lester C.
#495 Sautter, Albert P.
#496 Scott, Charles P.
#497 Scott, Irvin D.
#498 Vidal, Donald C.
#499 Wells, Verdie O.
#501 Corley, John K.
#502 Haynes, James R.

I believe the stay in Japan, for the most part, was rougher than it was in the Philippines because of the harder working conditions in the mines and the longer hours we had to work at it. Every day after twelve hours of working in the mine I spent my time either eating, taking a bath, or lying flat on my mattress in my room. I was so damn tired that I was never able to see the entire compound or visit with the men in the other shacks.

Cigarettes were always a problem in every camp I was in; Omine Machi was no different. The ration was one cigarette per man per week, unless one of the sergeants of the guard was hot about something and wouldn't even pass out that one cigarette per week. This wasn't a problem for me because I never did smoke cigarettes, although I did miss my daily cigars. Many of the men had a difficult problem because they thought they couldn't get by without their daily cigarettes, and I noticed many of them swapping their rice, soup, or bun, or even just a part of their food ration for extra cigarettes.

Although I didn't realize it, a buddy of mine, whom I had known for over three years and whose mattress was next to mine, had been trading his food for cigarettes for quite some time. I didn't notice it for quite awhile because he had always been thin, never being a muscular man even in peacetime. Several months had passed before I finally noticed that he was getting thinner and thinner, even more so than the rest of us. He had begun to look pale and weak to the point where there wasn't much left of him. I didn't want to see him starve himself, so one day I inquired as to whether he was trading his food for cigarettes. Not wanting to admit it, he replied, "No."

I believed him and let it pass for several more weeks until he began to appear even weaker. I then thought that he indeed must have been trading his food for cigarettes; so, to save his life, I grabbed him by the throat and pushed him against the wall. Squeezing his throat and making a point of speaking real rough to him, I said, "Bill, I don't believe you and I think you are trading." I then told him that if he didn't quit trading for cigarettes I would kill him. "Ok, ok, I will quit," he said, and apparently he really must have seen the light, because he lived to return to the States with the rest of us.

I've already mentioned that, always being hungry, we would steal the cabbages and onions that the guards grew throughout the compound. And really liking cabbage more than onions I would rather risk my life stealing them than the onions, even though stealing the onions was less dangerous. Well, I stole one head of cabbage too many and got caught doing it. For this I had hell to pay.

It had rained like hell on our walk back to the camp after working the night shift in the mine all night. We were all wet and coughing by the time we finally reached our shack. My buddy Bill and I sat on our mattresses talking about how nice a head of cabbage would taste. The nearest guard was sitting in a guard shack about fifty feet away directly opposite our end of the building. We figured that the guard would relax because of the rain—by this time it was raining quite heavily—thinking that nobody would attempt to escape in such a downpour. And sure enough, it appeared as though the guard was indeed taking a little nap because as he sat on his stool his head was bent forward and he had his rifle resting on top of his legs. So I told Bill to walk to the rear of our building and keep an eye on the guard and I would go and steal us a head of cabbage, which Bill did.

I waited several minutes before checking with Bill on the guard's position. When Bill gave me the ok sign, assuming the guard was dozing, I quickly looked around and saw a nice looking head of cabbage about six feet away. Barefoot and wearing only a pair of shorts, I jumped out of our room and pulled the head of cabbage out of the ground.

As soon as I had gotten the cabbage free I instinctively glanced towards the guard shack in order to see what the guard was doing. To my shock, he was looking directly at me, and within a moment was up and running towards me blowing his whistle for help. I quickly tossed the head of cabbage into our room and shouted for Bill to get rid of it, and then tried to cover the cabbage hole by kicking fresh dirt over and around it. By doing so I was hoping that the guards wouldn't be able to tell that I had stolen any of the cabbages; after all, with all the heavy rain, the entire compound was covered with water and mud.

I turned around just in time to see the guard, about six feet away, charging me with his bayonet pointing directly at my body. I raised my hands and then, with my right hand, pushed his rifle aside; his bayonet missing me by only a mere six inches. Having been running at me so fast and so hard, when he missed me the guard lost his balance and fell in the mud. I also lost my balance and likewise fell in the mud. I thought it best not to try to get up because by this time seven or eight other guards were also running towards me, and all where carrying their bayoneted-rifles. Nearly immediately I felt myself being hit with several rifle butts on all sides of my body. All the while I was being worked over by the guards I was trying to tell them that I hadn't taken a head of cabbage and was repeating, "*Ni, ni, ni,*" meaning no, no, no.

Finally, after I had taken about a hundred blows, they stopped beating me and I noticed that one of the guards was looking for the cabbage. Some of the fresh black dirt had fallen off the cabbage and onto the straw mat in my room when I had thrown the cabbage head to Bill. Poor little Bill must have been scared after the guards came at me. What he should have done was taken the head of cabbage and thrown it into the *benjo* at the end of the building. Nonetheless, the guard noticed the dirt and followed its trail to the other side of the building to where the head of cabbage lay. Upon finding it, the guard picked up the cabbage and brought it over to show it to me, which pretty much proved that I had stolen it. I was caught!

By this time I had stood up and a sergeant was hollering, "*Kiotski.*" With my entire body covered with mud, about five of the guards escorted me to the commandant's office. On the way they made it a point of slugging me a few more times.

The commandant was really angry. As I approached his desk, a sergeant gave a sharp command of *kiotski*, to which I obeyed, trying to stand as erect as possible. The commandant had a scowl on his face and was wearing dark glasses; it seemed as if a good three-fourths of the Japanese officers wore dark glasses. He pounded his fist on his desk and then began lecturing me in Japanese. He lectured me for about five minutes, stopping every minute or so to slap me across the face, at which time I would say, "*Hai, hai,*" which meant, "Yes, I agree with you." By this time in my captivity I knew that the Japs liked it if you said *hai* and agreed with them; it was something we nearly constantly heard them saying to each other. Although I understood very little of what the Commandant was saying, I still continued to repeat, "*Hai, hai,*" until he finally said, "*Koodo, koodo,*" meaning that the American should be taken out of his office.

I was immediately escorted from his office to a "Hot Box," which was located directly behind the guard shack at the main gate. The hot box was about two feet wide, five feet long, and two feet high. I was made to back into it in the prone position, having to lie flat with no room to turn around. I could only manage to turn over from my back to my stomach. Once inside, a guard snapped the padlock on the little square door. I thought at the time that this wouldn't be too rough, thinking I would just sleep all the while; but it soon turned out to be rougher than I thought.

Very little fresh air entered the box; the only air supply came from the door, which had eight two-inch square holes in it, and they didn't let much air in. It soon became very hot inside, and after several hours I began to sweat like a horse. I sweated so much inside the box that many times during my stay in it it seemed as if I was lying in a puddle of water. Because it had been very hot outside, I had been barefoot and only wearing a pair of shorts when I was caught; something which I was glad for, because it would have been even worse inside the box had I been wearing more clothes. I was also thankful that at least my head was at the front end by the air holes. In the evenings the slight breeze allowed a little more fresh air to filter in, and during the nights I found it wasn't as bad because the air was cooler and I didn't perspire as much as I did during the daylight hours when the hot sun shone down. It was, however, pitch dark in the box at night.

The box itself was constructed of two-inch hardwood planks. At first it was hard to rest on these boards and I twisted and turned a thousand times. I would first sleep on my back. When this began to hurt I would switch to my right side, then to my left side, finally turning onto my stomach, only to start all over again.

After about ten or twlve days on these boards I didn't mind it so much because I wasn't aware of what was taking place. I must have been on cloud nine and was probably even unconscious during most of my stay in the box because most of my memories of that time are only a blur. As an example, I don't remember eating or drinking anything during that time except eating the head of cabbage I had stolen; the Japs had given this to me at about 8 or 9 p.m. on the first night that I was in the box. I also don't remember asking for anything, nor do I think I would have.

I do recall that I had a thousand and one nightmares while in the box. I recall brief moments when I saw myself being beaten with fists and clubs by the Jap guards, and bleeding from many bayonet wounds. I recall waking up screaming and pounding on the little wooden door, and although faintly recalling hearing the guards occasionally talking, they always ignored my pleas. I recall that in many of my nightmares I talked to my family back in Maplewood, Wisconsin, and dreamed I was helping my father shoe horses and repair wagons in our old blacksmith shop like I had done as a kid. And I recall praying for hours on end for help and never giving up hope that I would survive all the punishment.

I remember that during my stay in the box, not once did I think about the stealing of the head of cabbage. I believe the reason for this was that I thought I didn't do anything wrong by stealing it because I was hungry, and I believe the Japs realized this, otherwise they wouldn't have given the cabbage head back to me.

One day I heard the noise of someone pounding on my little door. At first, I didn't pay any attention to the noise, but the pounding continued, becoming louder and louder. Finally, I heard someone speaking and recognized, "*Shi Shichi Go, Shi Shichi Go*, come here, come here."

At first I didn't believe that they were going to let me out of the box. I was in a frustrated state of mind, not knowing exactly where I was or what was happening to me. But, as the guard began pounding harder on the little door, I peered at it and slowly began to realize it was open. The guard repeated, "*Shi Shichi Go*, you come here," several more times until it finally dawned on me that I was being freed from my little box. The guard beckoned to me, indicating that I should crawl out. I managed to get myself out and staggered just beyond the guard shack, where I fell flat on my face. I struggled back to my feet, but again went down. One of my buddies saw me and called out to the others. Suddenly, I heard the voices of about 300 men cheering. The rest of the prisoners rushed towards me, picked me up, and carried me to my room. All the men crowded around my room and wondered how I was treated while in the hot box. I told them I didn't remember a hell of a lot, but that it was all a nightmare.

I wanted to know what had happened around the camp since I had gone into the hot box; whether anyone had been beaten up or shot, whether there had been any more war news. Our planes had been flying over the island and I was hoping there would be some favorable news and that it wouldn't be long before the war would end with the Japs' surrender. What I really wanted most, however, was a good drink of cold water; the good cold water that flowed from the nearby hills. Although not really hungry, and although not recalling eating anything except the head of cabbage while in the box, I asked the men what the menu was for dinner, to which they answered with the familiar rice, millet soup, and tea.

I was so damn weak—having sweated so much in the box, I realized I had lost about twenty pounds in there—but I didn't want to lie down.

After-all, I had just gotten up from lying in the prone position for too damn long of a period, so I slowly walked around the camp for about ten minutes in order to get my sea legs back.

Being finally let out of the box, the sunshine and daylight looked really beautiful to me. God must truly have been on my side; otherwise I wouldn't have survived this latest ordeal. One good thing I can say about my stay in the box, however, was that I at least had some much-needed rest while I was in it.

[How long Ed was actually in the hot box is left to conjecture. Ed mentions in his original memoirs that he thought he had been in it for "thirty days or so." This seems a very long time for anyone even in good physical shape to survive such an ordeal; much less someone in the shape Ed was in at the time. And, as Ed himself wrote, most of his "memories of that time are only a blur" and he was "on cloud nine and was probably even unconscious" during most of his stay in the box. The actual length of time Ed spent in the box is not truly relevant. His experiences in the box and the fact that he was able to overcome them and survive, however, is.]

10 Senso Wari – Our Captivity Ends

Surviving in any of the camps was a day to day ordeal. In our position we had to have a lot of guts and be willing to suffer extremely hard conditions if and when it became necessary. And we had to maintain our confidence at a high level at all times, as well as being ready at any time to help a friend in need. We also had to have a strong love for our country and be ready to die for it if needed.

Sometimes when we were punished by the Japanese we took it out on our friends, the same friends that we went through Bataan, Corregidor, and the several prison camps in the Philippines with. Our run down condition affected our minds; we experienced dizziness and headaches. We staggered when we walked. Some of us had illnesses and diseases and, as in my case, toes that were infected with fungi. We were also constantly hungry, which can do things to a man that nothing else can—it can be a strong motivator. Hunger pains gnaw at one's stomach, one's temperamental condition becomes very noticeable, and one easily gets disgusted. When a man's belly is empty and he gets desperate for food, the tendency always exists to give up completely—a dangerous tendency.

It took patience to withstand all the pressure. We had to possess certain qualities to refrain from striking back at our captors when they would punish us for the least of offenses with their brutal attacks. It took some time to understand our Japanese guards, and I tried to cooperate with them the best I could, but not to the extent that I would snitch on another American.

The punishments the guards dealt out were always harsh. Just for wiping our noses, four or five burly guards would beat us until we dropped. The Japs' forms of dealing out punishment varied with the disposition of the individual guard and his physical nature. A verbal outburst was the least one would receive; they became more severe from there. A face slapping; a hit in the face with fists; a hit in the back, rear end, or stomach with a rifle butt; having five or six guards taking turns slugged us in the face for about five minutes; being stripped to the shorts, made to stand with our hands above our heads while five or six guards took turns hitting our buttocks until they were busted open, stopping only when a blow to the kidneys felled us. More severe punishments were spending ten to thirty days in the hot box, being pierced by a bayonet, or being shot.

I saw all of these punishments dealt out and had to endure most of them myself. I actually believe the Japanese leaders attempted to instill hatred and disdain in the hearts of their own fighting men against us. Each individual prisoner had to possess a special determination to survive regardless of the punishment inflicted upon him, and every American that I witnessed took his punishment without a cry or a flinch. We knew our country was a great country and good to us, and we also knew that one day soon our fellow countrymen would come to rescue us.

I recall that several dozen times at the 4:15 a.m. *bango* at Omine Machi we had to recount and recount again numerous times because three or four men kept coming up with the wrong number two or three times in a row. And each time we would have to start over from the beginning. This would continue until we finally got the count right. Other times we had to wait, sometimes as long as five minutes, for a late man to show up before we could begin the count, and all the while during these counts it was usually cold as hell. I remember one morning during one of the *bangos* a man, who was late for the count, came running like crazy in my direction. He was so wild that I had to tackle him in an attempt to stop him. Although I was able to get him to the ground, I couldn't hold him by myself and it took a total of about five of us to finally hold him down. This type of thing happened from time to time. I believe the daily pressures were just too tough for some of the men to handle, and they just broke down mentally; after-all, the adverse pressures we were going through could get the best of men down. In cases like this, several Japanese guards would take over and we would never see the man again. I recall several times during the days while I worked the night shift that I saw the Japs carrying a box, which I was told contained an American body, to the top of a very high hill where, I was informed, the bodies would be cremated.

One element that was very necessary in surviving the prison camps was that of being able to get along with our fellow comrades under the very adverse conditions. I thought that about the worst possible act a friend could commit was that of theft, which happened to others and me from time to time during our captivity. I really believe, however, that most of the men were like me, feeling that to take food from another was the last thing they would ever do. If someone were in poor physical condition, his buddies would give him food, just like my buddies gave me food when I needed it. When one of our comrades stopped keeping themselves clean we would help them maintain good hygiene by giving them a bath with sand and water. Granted, this sounds cold and wasn't something we liked to do, but it was necessary for our comrades' own good. We had to stick together.

I was always ready to help my younger friends if they had a problem. I was older than many and had more experience in life, having ridden the rails, lived in hobo jungles, and spent over a year in the Civilian Conservation Camps prior to joining the Marine Corps. [Ed was twenty-five years old when he joined the Marine Corps, which would have made him about thirty-two years old in 1945. Most of the other men joined the Marines at age eighteen, which would make them in their mid-twenties at that time.] I also tried to settle arguments that would periodically arise between the men, many times being able to prevent fights and the unnecessary ill feelings they usually created.

In Japan we worked harder and longer than we had in the Philippines, the diet was just as insufficient, the beatings were more severe, and my thirty days in the hot box was almost intolerable. In addition, I don't think the dysentery I had acquired while in the different camps in the Philippines had ever completely left me, and no doubt this dysentery contributed to my rapid decline in weight in Japan. Other leftovers from the Philippines had followed us as well to Japan by way of nightmares; we seemed to be constantly dreaming of the many savage beatings that we had received while in the Philippines, not to mention those we were currently receiving.

After months of this kind of harsh treatment and living, one tended to adapt to the situation and just go along with the program; any suggestions of improvements to our condition just fell on deaf ears. Therefore, my philosophy during those 1,220 days of internment was to try to cooperate with my captors, obey their every command, and go along with their program while trying to stay as healthy as possible. This, however, as I've pointed out, didn't always work. In order to try and stay healthy, I had to go to the point of stealing food and, getting caught in doing so, paid for it. And even though attempting to obey the Japanese's every command, I still received countless beatings. Whenever I would fall while walking into or out of the coal mine, in order to help keep me going, I would always say to myself, "Get up and fight, you can't give up now after coming this far," or, "You know your mother is waiting for that phone call after you reach San Diego." It was a phone call that I did survive to make; God *was* on my side.

Although never knowing precisely what day or month it was without any access to calendars, the newspapers we were able to snatch from the old man in the mine provided us with hope. As I mentioned, in the early part of 1945 one of these newspapers indicated that the Japanese engaged American aircraft in dogfights over the Island of Honshu, the island we were on. This really lifted everyone's spirits because we began to believe the Americans were getting closer and the end of our captivity might truly be approaching.

Besides these dogfights, a further indication that the war wasn't going well for the Japanese was the actions of our guards in the lineups and formations while we were on the job in the mine. One of their favorite words they liked to use to get us to work faster was "*haiko*," which meant faster, and they began using it more and more often trying to get an extra carload of coal out of us every day, again pushing us until we just couldn't produce anymore. I told my buddies that we shouldn't do anything drastic that might irritate the Japanese because they might decide to shoot us, or, what I hated and feared even more, bayonet us. We all decided to continue to work as usual, and I made up my mind not to steal anymore cabbages; the hot box was just too rough.

One date that I recall well was the evening of 15 August 1945. I was sitting in my room that evening waiting for the 8 p.m. *bango*. I had the door open that was closest to and faced the fence and could easily hear the radios that were playing in the Japanese homes located next to the camp. At about 7:30 p.m., these radios began repeatedly announcing, "*Senso wari, senso wari*," which meant the war was over. I was immediately excited and overwhelmed, and ran down the ramp of the shack and told everyone what I had heard. They all quickly opened their doors and also began listening intently to the radios. It wasn't long before the whole camp was alerted and we all began to get the feeling that the end of our lengthy struggle of work and starvation was near. Although we hadn't yet received any word from the Japanese camp commander, official or otherwise, and we had to be careful not jump to conclusions too quickly, it was a tremendous relief to know that this horrible ordeal was about to end. The adrenaline was flowing with our anticipation of the end of our captivity, and I don't think anyone slept much that night.

As for me, it is impossible for me to put into words just exactly how I was feeling at that time. It wasn't long, however, before I began thinking about home and my return. I had not heard from my family for almost three years and I began to wonder what to expect when I would finally see them again. During my captivity I tried to keep my thoughts away from my family. I found that dwelling on my loved ones caused me to worry too much; thinking of them would have just made things that much harder. I made it a point just to pray each night that they would be safe.

Many of my buddies began getting worked up with excitement about the end arriving, so I told them to take it easy, thinking that if the news was actually true the Japanese guards might go berserk and start shooting; after-all, they still had their weapons. So, for the next several hours the radios blared away and everyone just listened and was happy as hell.

Each hour that passed began looking better for us. We all started to wonder if we would be marched off to the mine the next morning and began eagerly waiting for the normal 3:30 a.m. wake-up call to arrive to find out. One by one the hours passed by. Even though we thought the Jap leaders would hardly broadcast such a false statement and risk riling up the Japanese public, we were all still a bit nervous, thinking that the radio broadcasts might still be false; we still hadn't heard anything official from any of the Japanese.

We sat and talked all through the night; 3:30 a.m. came and went without a guard showing up to wake us. It was then that we figured the news was true, the war was over! We hugged and congratulated each other, and even began to holler out loud without giving a damn whether or not the Japanese heard us.

Looking towards the guard shack, I could see the guards were still sitting there, but very quiet, listless, and unconcerned about our actions. There was no doubt that they too had received the word, but these guards, these same guards that had beaten me unmercifully and put me in the hot box, these same guards that I wanted so desperately to kill the first chance I got, at the moment were still in control of us. Nonetheless, at that moment I was so happy that I completely forgot about wanting to kill them, and in talking to my buddies all we really wanted was to leave Omine Machi as soon as possible.

After 3:30 a.m. came and went, we waited until 4:30, then until 5:30, then 6:30, and finally at about 8 a.m. the Japanese camp commandant made an announcement informing us that the war was officially over and that the American Command had told him to await further orders.

All that day, 16 August, we did nothing but talk about how soon American forces would come in to take us out of Omine Machi and send us on our way back to the States. We just wanted to get out of Japan as quickly as possible and get some good American steaks and other food. We were told by one of our American officers that we could go over to the cook's shack where the cook would make us all the rice and soup we wanted. Many of us, including myself, decided we'd wait until the American forces arrived with either food or to take us to a place where we could get some real American food.

There wasn't a *bango* that day, nor would there ever be a *bango* again, and we talked in our rooms until about 1 a.m. We were quite sure that the following day would bring the American forces to rescue us, and, with that thought, we all finally decided to get some sleep.

Because we were so accustomed to our normal wake up time, we were all up and waiting the next morning at 3:30 a.m. It was 17 August. We went to the cook's shack and drank tea for several hours; sitting around talking about going home and wondering if our forces would be there today. But, because we were so far back in the hills of the mining area, we didn't know what to expect or by what method we would be leaving.

Finally, at about 9 a.m., we heard the sound of approaching airplanes. We hoped they were American, but, remembering how the Japanese strafed our positions on Corregidor while we flew white flags, we didn't want to take a chance, so we all ran back inside our shacks. A short time later, when the planes grew close enough for their wing insignias to be recognized, someone called out that they were B-29s. Within a few moments the planes began releasing several hundred, many different colored parachutes. What a wonderful sight to see!

Before the planes left they flew over the camp and dropped leaflets stating, "Good to see you," and, "Don't eat too much because we will be back tomorrow with more food." I had never seen a happier group of Americans; everyone was filled with joy and was smiling and laughing.

The parachutes dropped into the hills about a quarter of a mile from the camp. Happy and yelling, we quickly ran to them. Once there, each of us carried several of the boxes that the parachutes delivered back to the camp. Each of these boxes turned out to contain food, and it didn't take long for us to tear into them.

By this time the camp was in an uproar. Everyone was talking, laughing, and sampling all of the many different kinds of real American food that had just been dropped to us. The boxes contained milk, chocolate, cheese, candy, soups, crackers, and puddings, all of which looked so delicious to us. I can tell you that I had never been so happy since before the war. We sat on the floor-mats in our shacks and ate until we were filled, eating so much that we all had stomachaches.

That was probably the happiest day of my life up to that time, not only did I receive some real food, and a lot of it, but I finally realized the war was over. We would never again be forced to work twelve-hour shifts in the coal mines, we would never again go hungry, and we were soon to be going home to rest, eat good American food, and be reunited with our families.

On the following morning, 18 August, we were all still full from the large amount of food we had eaten the day before; we also slept late that morning. At about 9 a.m., just as they promised they would, we again heard the sound of airplanes overhead and saw that the B-29s had returned and were dropping more parachutes, which drifted down into the immediate area. This time, however, there was three times the amount of parachutes as the day before; these too were all filled with food. I later found out that the reason for dropping so much food was because the American High Command didn't know how many days it would be before they would be able to pick us up and transport us away, and they wanted to make sure we had enough food to last. After carrying all of this new batch of boxes back to the camp, every room had sufficient food to last for at least a full week.

Just like the day before, we began eating all this wonderful food. After three years and four months of eating only millet soup and rice, and precious little of either, one can only imagine how good this new supply tasted. The cook's shack supplied us with all the hot water we wanted for our food, and we lived like kings for two or three days.

Although there were more than a few stomachaches, no one really seemed to mind. We eventually solved this problem by eating for a little while, resting for a little while, and then eating some more. We would then lie down for about fifteen to twenty minutes, just to get up and try a different selection of food. I would have to say that I think every man ate too much, to the point of being uncomfortable. But we enjoyed every minute of it and just ate, rested, and loafed around talking about how wonderful it was to be finally free and to be an American. I must say at this point that I truly believe that all Americans do not fully realize just what a wonderful country we have with all of its freedoms.

I believe it was on 19 August 1945 when the American High Command contacted the camp at Omine Machi. I imagine the Japanese camp commander spoke to our highest-ranking officer, and they read the message together. It said that we were to get ready and that the Japanese were to take us to a designated rest camp where we would stay for several days.

Even after two or so days of almost constant eating, we still had more food than we could handle when the day finally arrived for us to leave the camp. We remembered an elderly Japanese man who had helped escort us to and from the mine and at times went down into the mine and acted like a straw boss. We remembered that he had never bothered any of us, was never angry at us, and treated us Americans like his own people, always giving us the time of day; he was just a good man.

I suppose you could say that Americans are always good for a soft touch and are always ready to share their blessings, because since we had so much food left over we told this old Japanese man to go and get his wagon and horse. When he returned, we filled his wagon high with boxes of our American food. In exchange, the old man hauled the food boxes that we were taking with us down to the train depot before we boarded the train to leave.

We were all happy as hell to be finally leaving the camp and walked to the railroad station where the old man was waiting for us with his wagon filled with our food boxes. As we boarded the train we each placed a box or two of food on the seats next to us for our convenience during the trip. Our train traveled most of the day, finally stopping before dark at a resort near the town of Omuta. When we left the train we carried our boxes of food along with us into the resort area.

Once at the resort we were assigned to eight-man shacks resembling hotels or motels back home. The shacks were very clean and were surrounded by green grass and large, tall shade trees. Each shack had several large sunken concrete tubs that were about six feet in diameter and oval in shape. These tubs contained water with a mixture of special minerals. Plenty of Japanese girls were available to serve us tea and hand out towels. These girls promised that if we spent enough time soaking in the mineral water we would quickly feel much better from our aches and pains. The girls were always ready to serve us tea, keep us cool with their beautiful fans, and provide hot water for our soup. Their objective was to keep us happy, content, and more or less help us heal our wounds. Besides bathing a lot, we spent plenty of time just resting on the straw-mated and quilt-covered floors, and relaxing and eating the food from the boxes we had received from the B-29s.

In reality, most of what I just wrote I remember only partially, because prior to finally landing in the States I must have been in somewhat of a daze. Try as I might I have not been able to fully remember all the incidents that occurred that first week to ten days after being liberated from the Omine Machi camp; it was probably the shock of being released after a horrible forty months in hell. Although the experiences of what happened prior to my capture in 1941 are so vivid, the experiences of what happened just after being released are almost blocked out. I heard later that our forces were so busy liberating prisoners from the many different Japanese POW camps that an American team was never able to accompany us to an evacuation point where we would have been given good physical and mental disorder examinations. [There were some 169 Japanese POW camps throughout the Japanese occupied territories. Like the POW camp at Omine Machi where Ed was, 127 of these were in the Japanese main islands.[40]]

After several days at this rest spot we were ready to leave and get back to San Diego for a good physical checkup and good American cooking. We packed what few belongings we had and boarded a train, which took us to Kanoya, Japan. When we arrived at the Kanoya station, we were taken directly to a large hotel where several doctors were to give us quick physical checkups. It was pitch dark when we arrived in Kanoya and once at the hotel there was no one to help us get oriented. As a result, I didn't know exactly where the hell I was that night and when I was told to strip down, I left my clothes on a chair along with a little packet that contained a diary that I had managed to carry with me throughout my three year ordeal. I went into the adjoining room for what turned out to be a very fast and incomplete quick going over rather than a physical, which went so damn fast that within two minutes I was back in the room where I had left my clothes and little packet.

To my shock and horror, I quickly noticed that my diary was gone. I could hardly believe that someone would steal such a treasure. I am positive to this day that another ex-POW, a Navy doctor, or pharmacist mate stole it. It was a dirty, low down trick, and I assure you that if I had caught the thief, I would have beaten him severely. They should have had military police or shore patrol stationed at the hotel to ensure the ex-prisoners were protected; after all, we weren't in very good physical shape. I placed a very high value on my diary because I risked being shot by the Japs if they had ever found it in one of the camps I had worked at, because I had written information in it that the Japs would have hated to read or have read by others.

Several times throughout that night my name was called with other names of men who were to leave for Guam, but I ignored each call, never answering. I wanted to find my diary, and I spent the rest of the night looking around the hotel, hoping I might catch the dirty S.O.B. who stole it. I walked around in a confused state of mind looking all through the hotel and inspected every bag that was open or appeared as though the person holding the bag might have had my diary. I never did find it. I had put so much effort into writing my diary and keeping it hidden from the Japanese and I was so damned mad at the loss of it that I cried.

About 8 a.m. the next morning I decided that I wouldn't find the culprit and checked with a Navy officer about a lift to Guam. He steered me to an L.S.T. [Tank Landing Ship, also pronounced Landing Ship, Tank], which I was told had been converted to transport us weary, beaten, thin, injured, bony, but very happy Marines and sailors back home. While on my way to Guam I was treated like a long lost dog. The Navy crew served me steak and ice cream, the first of both I had had since early 1941. I was now feeling better, not physically, but mentally, because I was on my way home, first to Guam, then to San Diego, then to Wisconsin. Although I was still angry about losing my diary, I knew that the memories were still engrained in my mind, so I took some comfort in knowing that I could reproduce the diary's contents at a later time.

Immediately after our arrival in Guam we were bussed to the hospital for another check-up. The hospital on Guam was the first United States hospital we entered since before our surrender and the doctors were better equipped to perform the type of tests and examinations that we needed. After what proved to be our most complete and thorough examination since our release, we were told we could tour the island.

I was really amazed at the many changes the island had incurred since I had stopped there in 1939 en route to Shanghai. Although during that first brief visit to Guam we had only been able to go ashore for just one afternoon and spent much of that time drinking beer, consequently not seeing a lot of the island, it had appeared to have nothing but dirt roads and a lot of jungle. Now the island was a network of concrete roads and numerous steel buildings containing military equipment. There were also numerous ships in the harbor and a lot of aircraft parked on the airfield. I could hardly believe it was the same place.

We stayed in Guam for two days, after which we headed for San Diego and the naval hospital there. Once at the hospital in San Diego we underwent additional tests and physical examinations to determine the extent of our conditions and for the need of further treatment. The doctors there gave us a very thorough examination, including x-rays and taking blood, urine, and stool samples. Because of all the injuries I had sustained—smashed foot, gashed leg, fungi infected toes, shots in 1942 and 1944 by the Japs using un-sterile needles, working barefoot in water while my feet bled—and all the unsafe food we sometimes ate—pork from the hogs that had been dead for two or three days; dead, smelly fish that had washed ashore—the doctors thought there was something wrong with my blood, so they gave me fifty shots of penicillin.

While at the San Diego Naval Hospital we were well treated. The nurses were the finest and were always very understanding, and, while waiting for the results of the many tests, we were given open gate liberty, which meant we could come and go as we pleased unless notified that we needed to see a doctor for treatment or more tests. We were never reprimanded, no matter how late we stayed out at night. The first place we visited was a restaurant that served good old steaks. It felt so different to sit in a booth and have a pretty waitress wait on us, to have silver utensils to eat with, and to have table cloths covering our tables. We had salt and pepper, potatoes, gravy, vegetables, and a desert, and we were all dressed to kill and even tipped the pretty waitress that served us. I remember it was one of our first good meals since 1941.

After finishing all of my medical tests, the doctors told me that I could go home for a visit and then to report to the naval hospital at the Great Lakes Naval Base in Illinois for further treatment. I hadn't been home since I left on 20 December 1938 and was very happy to receive the word that I could go. I ran to the nearest telephone and called my mother telling her the good news. I told her I would travel by train and expected to arrive in Green Bay, Wisconsin, about 10 p.m. three days from that day, which would be 16 November 1945, and that I would meet her and my family at the Green Bay Y.M.C.A.

I didn't sleep very well on the trip home because I began to wonder how many members of my family were still living. I had not received any word or notice since 1942. All of my time during these many days in captivity was taken up by either working, marching to or from work, eating what little we were given, bathing, or trying to get whatever sleep I could. I had lived one day at a time, never knowing what that day or the next would bring, whether I would have to go through another beating, or whether I would lose control and hit a guard. All of this left little time to dwell on my family, which was just as well. As I've mentioned, however, I did find time to pray for them each night.

Besides thinking of my family, I spent most of the rest of the time on the train thinking about the ordeal that I had just gone through: the big black snakes, the beatings, stealing food while trying not to get caught, working barefoot while my feet bled. When I was able to sleep on the train, however, I had nightmares about my ordeal. I dreamt about smashing my foot on the Manila docks, the Hell Ship, and my bleeding and fungi infected toes. I was in an upper berth and must have done a lot of talking in my sleep and made a lot of trips to the toilet, because I think I must have worried some of the other passengers on the train. I bet the porter thought, "What the hell is wrong with this Marine? He must have really been in Hell."

During the daytime a great number of people wanted to talk with me. They wanted to know where I had spent my time during the war. But I was reluctant to talk about the living hell I had just returned from. I was on my way to meet my family, and I really just wanted to be left alone. So, between this and still being somewhat nervous about meeting my family again, I spent quite a few hours drinking by myself in the dining car.

Green Bay, Wisconsin, had a special place in my heart because I had both worked and fought a lot of boxing bouts as an amateur boxer there before the war. I also had many personal friends in the city; plus my family would be waiting for me there, so I was very anxious to reach it. At about 9:30 p.m. on 16 November 1945 my train finally pulled into the Green Bay station. I took a cab to the Y.M.C.A. and paced the floor of the lobby until about 10 p.m. when my folks walked through the door. Although it had been almost six years, we recognized each other immediately and I embraced each of them.

We talked for several minutes, and I then suggested we walk across the main street and have a few welcome home drinks. Since I was anxious to go home and see the place that I had many times never expected to see again, after just a few drinks we left the bar for home. We arrived in Maplewood about 11:30 p.m., and to see my home again, after living in bamboo shacks in the Philippines and the clapboard shacks in Japan, was like seeing heaven.

Almost immediately, my mother broke out some good, homemade coffeecake and grade-A milk. We then all sat around the dining room table and talked about what everyone was doing at the time and what had happened during the six years I was gone. It was then that I learned that a dozen or more relatives and friends had died.

Although I wanted to hear about the events that happened at home, I didn't want to talk about my experiences, at least not at that time. All I said was that it was very rough and that I was lucky to be alive and happy to be home. I realized that there were many things about my stay in the hands of the Japanese that I wouldn't want my mother and sisters to hear about, and to this day I have never related to them all the narrow escapes with death that I had. I decided not to tell my friends about the war either, because one has to go through something like I had just gone through to be able to comprehend exactly what occurred, and I didn't think they would understand or even believe what I would tell them.

For about the next six months all I wanted to do was relax. I wanted to be able to sleep late and not have to get up for *bango* or be forced to do anything I didn't want too do. I just wanted to sleep as late as I chose, smoke cigars, and drink beer, and to be able to do these things whenever I wanted to.

At about 4:30 a.m. that first night I went to my old room and my old bed with its spring mattress and clean white sheets. It was so relaxing slipped between the two sheets that I quickly fell fast asleep.

I was in no hurry the next morning to get up, so I didn't. Not until about 11 a.m. did I go downstairs to wash. After washing I immediately smelled hot coffee brewing and sat down to a real breakfast, which included a large glass of orange juice, six fresh fried eggs, fried potatoes, four slices of toast with strawberry jam, dry cereal with fresh milk, and all the hot coffee I wanted. I will never have a meal of *lugao* and tea again. I said my prayer and ate.

I had no more than finished my breakfast when a family who had been our family friends for many years came over for a short visit. I was really surprised when they presented me with a wallet to hold all of my back pay, a beautiful ring, and a card signed by every one of their relatives that lived in the area. These were real true friends, and it was a gesture that I will never forget as long as I live. In addition to this family, another person that I will never forget is a first cousin of mine who took the time to write a letter that I received while I was a prisoner in the Philippines. He was the only person beside my sister who took the time to write me while I was interned.

I stayed at my family home in Maplewood for about six months. I needed the rest and time to regain some of my strength and weight that I had lost during my captivity. I didn't go to the village to help my father in the blacksmith shop until I had enough strength back that I could be of some help to him. I hadn't realized just how much strength I had actually lost until I tried to do some work around the family farm. I was also reluctant to be seen by my friends that I had known for years, thinking that they would be surprised at seeing me in the condition I was in.

I soon realized that it might take longer than I had anticipated to become adjusted to my old normal ways of living. Spending over six years living and working amongst the Chinese, Filipinos, and Japanese affected my actions, both mentally and physically—my thinking, viewpoints, language, and all around behavior. It also seemed as though I wanted to be alone more now than I did before I had left home to join the Marines. And there were quite a number of people that I didn't feel as if I wanted to speak to because their outlooks on life were now so much different than mine.

One day during my stay at home my mother showed me a card she had received in 1943 from the Imperial Japanese Army. This card had been given to me by the Japanese and I had to underline certain sentences and add a few statements; statements which would have no affect on the status of the preprinted underlined sentences. A sample of the card is as follows [the words in parenthesis are those that were underlined by Ed]:

I am interned at Prison Camp #10 D Philippines.
My health is poor, fair, good, (excellent).
I am (uninjured), in hospital, under treatment, not under treatment.
I am improving, not improving, better, (well).
Please see that Dad, brothers and sisters are notified.
Keep both farms.
Please give my regards to everyone.
To: Mrs. Ferd Babler, Maplewood, Wisconsin, U.S.A.

[Ed was allowed to send only three of these post card size preprinted cards during his 1,220 days of captivity.]

After thirty-five years of trying to erase from my mind the many atrocious acts the Japanese conducted against me, the memories are still very vivid. The Japanese considered POW camps as extensions of battlefields and those prisoners contained in these camps as enemies to be fought. It should be noted that after General Wainwright was forced to surrender all American and Filipino forces in the Philippines, the Japanese dive-bombers still bombed my gun position on Corregidor. The Japanese troops must have known that we had surrendered, white flags had gone up all over the place, but they still bombed both my position and others near me.

I still have bitter memories about my treatment as a POW. I can still vividly recall the many beatings, the Hell Ship, the many months of working barefoot, my toes being crushed by the barrel of cement, my leg operation, and the hot box. I still remember the march through Manila and the sounds of the gun shots, knowing that a fellow American had just been shot for falling out of line. I still remember watching my friends and fellow prisoners die from malaria and dysentery. I still remember those four men who had walked away from the camp in Cabanatuan, and seeing them shot while standing over the holes they had just been forced to dig for their own graves. I remember the false promises given to us of better food for harder work to get us to volunteer to go to Palawan. I remember almost dying from pleurisy until a Japanese doctor gave me pills and milk, saving my life. I will never forget working in the coal mine in Japan, almost constantly hitting my head on the beams. I still remember the Jap lover who caused me so much extra work. I still remember the lack of food and having to risk being beaten, or worse, by stealing food to survive.

I still remember.

Epilogue

After being release from the POW camp, Ed, like most of his fellow ex-POWs, was promoted to the next pay grade and given all the back pay owed to him, minus deductibles. Within a year or two after their release the United States Government also gave all the former Japanese held POWs $1 for each day they were held captive and later $1.50 for each day they performed hard labor as POWs. For Ed's 1,220 days in Japanese captivity his share of this extra pay added up to about $3,050.00.

As soon as it was possible, Ed went to the Great Lakes Naval Base in Illinois just north of Chicago where, on 16 March 1946, he received an honorable discharge. He was soon after able to gain employment at a shipyard in Manitowoc, Wisconsin, where he met Jeanette Rochon, a native from Two Rivers, Wisconsin. They were married in May 1947 and, less than a month later, Ed was accepted, ironically, as a prison guard at the Wisconsin State Maximum-Security Prison in Waupun, Wisconsin. Ed and Jeanette moved to Waupun in June of 1947 where Ed worked at the prison as a guard and later as an industries technician for the next twenty-six years until his health became so bad that he was forced to retire on full disability. While in Waupun, Ed started a boxing club and trained young men for the Golden Gloves, four of which made it to the finals in Milwaukee.

In the mean time, Ed and Jeanette had two sons, Joseph and John. Both sons joined the military and served in Vietnam, Joe in the Army and John in the Marine Corps. Joe received two Purple Hearts. Joe's daughter, Ed's and Jeanette's granddaughter, also joined the military, spending six years in the Marine Corps.

For his many sacrifices and personal indignities suffered for his country during World War II, Marine Sergeant Edmond Babler was awarded the Bronze Star Medal, the United States Marine Corps Medal, the Bataan-Corregidor Medal, the World War II Victory Medal, the Prisoner of War Medal, the American Defense Ribbon, and the Asiatic Pacific Campaign Ribbon. However, Ed had also suffered numerous injuries at the hands of his Japanese captors, and as such felt he deserved the Purple Heart Medal. Personally applying many times for this award, Ed was always told that there was simply not enough evidence with which to prove he had received wounds at the hands of the Japanese.[41]

Ed passed away on 29 January 1994. Father Benjamin Knopp's eulogy fittingly summarized Ed's life:

> Ed Babler was a tough guy.
>
> He had to be a tough guy to beat the Navy Boxing Champ on the ship on the way to the Philippines.
> But his victory over the Navy Boxing Champ was child's play over what he would have to endure a short time later. Perhaps it was, in some way, a preparation for it.
>
> Ed Babler HAD to be a tough guy to survive three years and four months as a prisoner-of-war.
> No one endured more brutal treatment at the hands of his Japanese captors that he did, and lived to tell it.
>
> Ed Babler HAD to be a tough guy to win the Bronze Star, for bravery and courage.
> They don't give Bronze Stars to panty-waists!
>
> Ed's favorite poem, and it had a great deal of meaning for him, was written by a nameless author, found on a jury-rigged grave-marker near Lunga Point, Guadalcanal. It reads:
>
>> And when he gets to Heaven,
>> To St. Peter he will tell,
>> "One more Marine reporting, Sir,
>> I've served my time in Hell."

Ed Babler WAS a tough guy.
But Ed Babler was ALSO a gentle man, a kind man, a loving man, a generous man, a good man.

He was a devoted and faithful husband, and a loving father to his sons.

He was employed for 26 years at the Wisconsin State Prison where he was respected by his fellow guards and by the inmates as well. Having been a prisoner himself, he had a certain empathy for the prisoners like no one else could have. . . .

. . . At the end of his long life, Ed Babler can fittingly say for himself:

"I have fought the good fight,
I have finished the course,
I have kept the faith.
For the rest,
there is laid up for me a crown of glory,
which the Lord, the just judge,
will give me on that day."[42]

As heart rending and horrific as Ed's story is, it is, unfortunately, not a unique one. Some 50,000 American POWs, both military and civilian, suffered through similar brutalities at the hands of the Japanese soldier and civilian alike while held in 169 known Japanese POW and civilian internment camps spread throughout the Japanese occupied lands and islands during World War II.[43] Like Ed, those who survived to come home were the lucky ones. From 1941 to 1945, nearly 40 percent of the United States military prisoners died while in Japanese captivity; this compared to the 1 percent that died in the hands of the Nazis.[44]

Ed was one of approximately 25,000 American prisoners sent to work in Japanese owned and operated factories, mines, and shipyards in Japan.[45] Of the 55,279 Japanese held POWs from all nations transported by sea to Japan, Formosa, China, and Korea, 10,853 drowned en route when the unmarked Hell Ships they were being transported in were torpedoed or bombed, and at least another 500 perished from disease and thirst; 3,632 of these were American.[46] Of the 1,487 members of the 4th Marine

Regiment that surrendered on Corregidor that fateful day in May 1942, 474 did not come home from the Japanese POW camps.[47]

The Japanese Imperial Army considered it dishonorable for a fighting man to surrender to the enemy, expecting them to either fight to the death or commit suicide. On 8 January 1942, General Hideki Tojo, Japanese Minister of War, issued a Field Service Code order setting forth the way Japanese military and civilian personnel were to view and treat POWs, stating that "To live as a prisoner of war is to live without honor." To the Japanese, life without honor was a worthless existence, and the POWs were to be treated and cared for as worthless.[48]

It was not until nearly seven years after his death, and then only through the tireless efforts of his widow, Jeanette, and letters of affidavits by friends and fellow POWs like John M. Emerick,[49] James Carrington,[50] Donald Vidal,[51] and Cliff Omtuedt[52] that Ed Babler was finally awarded his well-deserved Purple Heart, posthumously. On 11 November 2000, Veterans Day, Marine Corps Major John O'Brien, accompanied by an honor guard from Golf Company, Marine Forces Reserve in Madison, Wisconsin, presented Jeanette Babler with Ed's Purple Heart Medal in a ceremony at the home of Ed's and Jeanette's oldest son in Lamartine, Wisconsin. A headline in the next day's local newspaper read, "Waupun Marine earns Purple Heart – posthumously." Under the headline, fittingly, yet belated, appeared a tribute to Edmond Babler, U.S. Marine, World War II veteran, survivor of Corregidor, survivor of 1,220 days in brutal Japanese prisoner of war camps, and American hero.[53]

About the Author

Robert C. Daniels grew up in Waupun, Wisconsin. After graduating from Waupun Senior High School with the class of 1976, he joined the Navy to see the world. Upon his eventual retirement from the service, after indeed seeing quite a bit of the world, he attended and graduated from Old Dominion University in Norfolk, Virginia, with a BA in History and the American Military University in Manassas Park, Virginia, with an MA in Military Studies. He currently lives in Chesapeake, Virginia, with his wife and their cherished pets where he teaches adjunct History courses at the Virginia Beach campus of Tidewater Community College and online courses at the University of Phoenix. He is also the author of several military history articles published online at militaryhistoryonline.com.

Selected Bibliography

Cited Works

Center for Research: Allied POWS under the Japanese. "American Roster Omine Machi POW Camp." http://www.mansell.com/pow_resources/camplists/fukuoka/fuku_5_omine/yanks_fuku_5.html, accessed on 9 November 2007.

_____ "Omine, Fukuoka Camp #5-B." http://www.mansell.com/pow_resources/camplists/fukuoka/fuku_5_omine/fuku_5_omine.html, accessed on 9 November 2007.

Babler, Edmond J. "1220 Days In Hell," Waupun, Wisconsin.

Holmes, Linda Goetz. *Unjust Enrichment: How Japan's Companies Built Postwar Fortunes Using American POWs*. Mechanicsburg, PA: Stackpole Books, 2001.

Keegan, John. *The Second World War*. New York: Penguin Books, 1990.

Kerr, E. Bartlett. *Surrender and Survival: The Experience of American POWs in the Pacific 1941-1945*. New York: William Morrow and Company, Inc., 1985.

Knopp, Father Benjamin. Eulogy: "Funeral: Edmond Babler, 2 February1994."

Knox, Donald. *Death March: The Survivors of Bataan*. New York: Harcourt Brace & Company, 1981.

Miller, J. Michael. *From Shanghai to Corregidor: Marines in the defense of the Philippines*. Washington D.C.: Marine Corps Historical Center, 1997.

Morris, Eric. *Corregidor: The American Alamo of World War II*. New York: First Cooper Square Press, 2000.

The Reporter (Fond du Lac, Wisconsin), 12 November 2000.

Office of the Provost Marshal General. *Report on American Prisoners of War Interned by the Japanese in the Philippines*, 1945.

Wright, John M. *Captured on Corregidor: Diary of an American P.O.W. in World War II*. Jefferson, NC: McFarland & Company, Inc., 1988.

Zimba, John Patrick. Personal interview by author, 3 Feb 2001.

Uncited Works

Daws, Gavan. *Prisoners of the Japanese: POWs of World War II in the Pacific*. New York: William Morrow and Company, Inc., 1994.

Grady, Frank J. and Rebecca Dickson. *Surviving the Day: An American POW in Japan*. Annapolis, MA: Naval Institute Press, 1997.

Lawton, Manny. *Some Survived*. Chapel Hill, NC: Algonquin Books of Chapel Hill, 1984.

Morrison, Samuel Eliot. *History of United States Naval Operations in World War II*. Vol. 3, *The Rising Sun in the Pacific, 1931-April 1942*. Boston: Little, Brown and Company, 1984.

Villarin, Mariano. *We Remember Bataan and Corregidor: The Story of the American & Filipino Defenders of Bataan and Corregidor and Their Captivity*. Baltimore, MD: Gateway Press, Inc., 1990.

Notes

1. John Keegan, *The Second World War* (New York: Penguin Books, 1990), p. 265.
2. Ibid., p. 266.
3. Eric Morris, *Corregidor: The American Alamo of World War II* (New York: First Cooper Square Press, 2000), p. 51.
4. Michael J. Miller, *From Shanghai to Corregidor: Marines in the defense of the Philippines* (Washington D.C.: Marine Corps Historical Center, 1997), p. 1.
5. Morris, p. 51.
6. Ibid., p. 53.
7. Miller, p. 3.
8. Ibid., pp. 1-3.
9. Ibid., p. 7.
10. Morris, pp. 119-120.
11. Miller, p. 8-9.
12. Morris, p. 136.
13. Ibid., p. 137.
14. Miller, p. 9.
15. Ibid., p. 8.
16. Ibid., p. 14.
17. Ibid., pp. 6-10.

18. Ibid., pp. 13-14.
19. Ibid., p. 18.
20. Ibid., p. 19.
21. Morris, p. 31.
22. Miller, p. 41.
23. Ibid., p. 42.
24. *Report on American Prisoners of War Interned by the Japanese in the Philippines* (Office of the Provost Marshal General, 1945).
25. Linda Goetz Holmes, *Unjust Enrichment: How Japan's Companies Built Postwar Fortunes Using American POWs*, (Mechanicsburg, PA: Stackpole Books, 2001), p. 44-45.
26. E. Bartlett Kerr, *Surrender and Survival: The Experience of American POWs in the Pacific 1941-1945* (New York: William Morrow and Company, Inc., 1985), p. 87.
27. Ibid., pp. 212-215.
28. John M. Wright, *Captured on Corregidor: Diary of an American P.O.W. in World War II* (Jefferson, NC: McFarland & Company, Inc., 1988), p. 69.
29. Holmes, p. 12.
30. Miller, p. 19.
31. Holmes, p. 158-159.
32. Ibid., p. 154.
33. Ibid., p. 158.
34. Donald Knox, *Death March: Survivors of Bataan* (New York: Harcourt Brace & Company, 1981), p. 365.
35. Center for Research: Allied POWS under the Japanese, "Omine, Fukuoka Camp #5-B" (http://www.mansell.com/pow_resources/camplists/fukuoka/fuku_5_omine/fuku_5_omine.html, accessed on 9 November 2007).
36. Knox, p. 365.
37. Ibid., p. 441.
38. Holmes, pp. xxi and 149.

39. Center for Research: Allied POWS under the Japanese, "American Roster Omine Machi POW Camp" (http://www.mansell.com/pow_resources/camplists/fukuoka/fuku_5_omine/yanks_fuku_5.html, accessed on 9 November 2007).

40. Ibid., p. 27.

41. Frank Scotello, "Waupun Marine earns Purple Heart – posthumously," (*The Reporter* Fond du Lac, Wisconsin), 12 November 2000.

42. Father Benjamin Knopp. Eulogy: "Funeral: Edmond Babler, 2 February 1994."

43. Holmes, pp. xvii and 27.

44. Ibid., p. xvii.

45. Ibid., p. xvii.

46. Ibid., p. 33.

47. Miller, p. 42.

48. Holmes, p. 12.

49. John M. Emerick spent two years with Ed on the Philippine Island of Luzon at the POW camps at Zeblon Field and Nielsen Field.

50. James Carrington, also known as "Frenchy the Cajun," was with Ed at Nielsen Field in the Philippines. He eventually escaped from Bilibid Prison in Manila and fought with the Philippine guerrilla forces for the remainder of the war, for which he received numerous awards and medals from both the U.S. Army and Marine Corps.

51. Don Vidal was onboard the Noto Maru with Ed, as well as with him at Shanghai, China and the Omine Machi camp in Japan.

52. Cliff Omtuedt helped Ed during the period when Ed suffered through his serious leg injury. Cliff passed away in June 2000.

53. Scotello.

Index

Index

A
Adams, Lieutenant Colonel John P. 14, 149
Amerant, Raymond J. 118
American Defenders of Bataan and Corregidor (ADBC) 40, 70, 73
American Defense Ribbon 142
American Engineers 106
Army Air Corps 115
Asiatic Pacific Campaign Ribbon 142
Axis Powers xvi

B
B Company, 1st Battalion Fleet Marine Force, Sixth Marine Force 1, 4, 9
B-17 Bombers xiv
B-29 Bombers 130, 131, 133
Babler, Ferdinand xix
Babler, Jeanette vii, xi, 65, 70, 93, 144
Babler, John 74, 141
Babler, Joseph 74, 141
Babler, Katherine xix
Baguio, Region of Luzon 65
Baker, Roger D. 118
Bataan-Corregidor Medal 142
Bataan Death March xvi
Bataan Peninsula xiv, xv, 21, 22, 26, 55, 147, 148, 150
Battery Geary 26
Battery Way 26
Bilibid Prison 35, 54, 67, 70, 86, 87, 92, 151
Blood Alley 5
Blue Lake, Wisconsin xix
Bronze Star Medal 142
Brussels High School xix
Bubbling Well Road 6
Bund 3, 13

C
Cabanatuan 31, 36, 38, 39, 40, 41, 53, 55, 88, 92, 139
Carrington, James 70, 144, 151
Cavite Navy Yard 14, 17, 18, 20, 21
CCC. *See* Civilian Conservation Corps xix
Chicago, Illinois 1, 69, 141
Chinese xvi, 3, 5, 6, 8, 9, 10, 11, 12, 13, 138
Chinese Marines xvi
Churchill, British Prime Minister Winston xvi
Civilian Conservation Corps xix
Clement, Lieutenant Colonel William T. 23
Coolies 10, 13, 118

Corley, John K. 119
Corregidor v, vii, xiv, xv, xvi, 16, 21, 22, 23, 24, 25, 26, 27, 28, 30, 32, 33, 38, 40, 55, 70, 73, 79, 86, 125, 130, 139, 142, 144, 147, 148, 149, 150

D

D Company, 1st Battalion, 4th Marine Regiment 23
Door County xix
Duncan, Louis E. 79, 118

E

Eau Claire, Wisconsin 65
Emerick, John M. 144, 151
English 5, 8, 34, 42, 67, 80, 82, 101
Etter, Frank G. 119
European first strategy xv

F

Ferry Road 4
Filipino Army xv
1st Separate Marine Battalion 14, 20, 21, 22, 23, 86
Fischer, Culver L. 119
Fisher, George N. Jr. 119
Formosa, Island of xiii, 143
Fort Drum 25
Fort Hughes 27
4th Marine Regiment vii, xvi, 4, 5, 8, 9, 12, 17, 22, 23, 28, 86, 108, 144
Furukawa Mining 102

G

Gilbertson, Homer A. 119
Golden Glove xix, 72, 141
Golf Company, Marine Forces Reserve 74, 144
Graigg, Thomas R. 119
Great Lakes Naval Base 135, 141
Green Bay, Wisconsin 69, 135, 136
Guadalcanal, Island of 142
Guam, Island of 134, 135

H

Hall, Major 2
Hamby, Thornton E. 118
Hart, Admiral Thomas 23
Hathorne, Walter W. 118
Hawaii xiii, xiv, 2
Hayden, Doctor 77, 78, 79, 80
Haynes, James R. 119
Henderson 2, 3, 13
Hesler, James C. 118
Hiroshima xii, 97
Homma, General Masaharu, Japanese xiv, xv, xvi
Honshu, Island of xii, 97, 114, 115, 128
Hot Box 86, 121, 122, 123, 124, 126, 127, 128, 129, 139
Howard, Colonel Samuel L. 5, 23, 29

I

Imperial Japanese Army 138
Italian Marines 6, 7

J

Japan xii, xvi, 4, 33, 46, 64, 80, 86, 87, 91, 92, 93, 94, 97, 99, 100, 102, 111, 114, 115, 119, 127, 130, 133, 137, 139, 143, 147, 148, 150, 151

K

Kanoya, Japan 133
King, General Edward xvi
Knopp, Father Benjamin 142, 147, 151
Koreans 10
Kyushu, Island of xii, 97

L

La Jolla, California 1
Lamartine, Wisconsin 74, 144
Lang, William J. 118
Latham. John D. 118
Lee, Charles R. 118
Little Club 7
Lunga Point 142

Luzon, Island of xiv, xv, 15, 17, 19, 20, 22, 23, 84, 86, 151

M

MacArthur, General Douglas xiv, xv, xvi, 23, 24, 29, 54
Madison, Wisconsin 17, 74, 144
Manila xiv, xv, 2, 14, 20, 22, 24, 31, 32, 33, 34, 35, 36, 37, 38, 41, 42, 46, 54, 55, 56, 64, 67, 68, 69, 70, 71, 83, 85, 87, 93, 94, 136, 139, 151
Manitowoc, Wisconsin 141
Maplewood, Wisconsin xix, 55, 92, 123, 136, 138
Mare Island Navy Base 2
Mariveles Naval Base 17, 21, 23
Matheny, Wilfred R 118
Mc Clung, William J. 118
McDavitt, Captain Jerome 101
McKinley Field 45, 55, 56, 57, 59, 64, 92
Meyers, Malvern R. 118
Milwaukee, Wisconsin 67, 69, 141
Minneapolis, Minnesota 7
Mitsubishi 93

N

Nagumo, Admiral Chichi, Japanese xiii
Nanking Road 3
Naval Hospital, Great Lakes, Illinois 135
Naval Hospital, San Diego, California 135
Nazis 143
New Orleans, Louisiana 70
Nielsen Field 59, 60, 61, 62, 64, 65, 66, 67, 68, 69, 70, 71, 72, 77, 82, 84, 92, 151
Nippon Yusen 93
Noto Maru 92, 93, 151

O

O'Brien, Major John 144
Olongapo Navy Yard 17

Omine Machi xii, 86, 97, 98, 100, 101, 102, 103, 105, 106, 108, 109, 111, 112, 114, 117, 118, 119, 126, 130, 132, 133, 147, 151
Omtuedt, Clifford 65, 151
Omuta 132
Orange Plan xiv, xv

P

Palace Cabaret 6
Palawan 42, 43, 45, 46, 47, 48, 49, 51, 53, 54, 55, 60, 64, 84, 92, 112, 113, 117, 139
Panginay 36
Pearl Harbor xiii, xiv, 17, 23, 26
Philippine Army xiv
Philippine Islands xiii, xiv, xvi, xix, 13, 17, 22, 27, 29, 30, 33, 41, 51, 55, 86
Philippine Scouts Division xiv, 33
Pitzel, Daniel J. 118
Pleurisy 51, 54, 64, 84, 92, 112, 117, 139
Prisoner of War Medal 142
Puerto Princesa 43
Purple Heart Medal 74, 142, 144, 151

Q

Quezon, Philippine President Manuel Luis Quezon Antonia y Molino 24

R

Red Cross 54
Richter, A. 118
Roosevelt, President Franklin Delano xv
Russell, William J. 10, 119
Russians 5, 7, 8, 9, 13
Ruzek, Lester C. 119

S

San Diego, California xix, 1
San Diego Naval Hospital 135
Sangley Point 14, 19, 20
Sangley Point Radio Station 19

Sautter, Albert G. 119
Sayre, U.S. Commissioner Francis Bowes 24
Scott, Charles F. 119
Scott, Irvin C. 119
2nd Battalion, 4th Marine Regiment 23
Shanghai, China xvii, xix, 1, 2, 3, 4, 5, 6, 7, 8, 9, 12, 13, 17, 38, 40, 60, 86, 108, 109, 118, 134, 147, 149, 151
Shimoko, Lieutenant 39
Sixth Marine Force 1
Smith, Raymond E. 119
Soochow Creek 4, 9, 10, 12
Spinal Arthritis 105
SS President Harrison 17
SS President Madison 17
Star Lake xix
Strickland, Eldon K. 119
Supreme Court 112
Sutherland, General Richard K. 23

T

Taylor, Jack 9, 40
3rd Battalion, 4th Marine Regiment 28
Tojo, General Hideki, Japanese Minister of War 71, 115, 144
Turner, Gerald A. 118
24th Field Artillery Philippine Scouts 101
Two Rivers, Wisconsin 141

U

UCLA 67
United States Air Force 115
United States Marine Corps Medal 142
United States War College xiv
Upper Peninsula of Michigan xix

V

Veterans Administration 67
Vidal, Donald C. 119, 144, 151
Vietnam 141
Vinson, Benjamin H. 119

W

Wainwright, General Jonathan xvi, 29, 30, 139
War Plan 5 xvi
Waupun, Wisconsin 66, 67, 141, 144, 145, 147, 151
Wells, Verdie O. 119
Whangpoo River 4
Wisconsin xix, 1, 36, 55, 65, 66, 67, 69, 74, 92, 113, 123, 134, 135, 136, 138, 141, 143, 144, 145, 147, 148, 151
Wisconsin State Maximum-Security Prison 141
World War II Victory Medal 142

Y

Y.M.C.A. 135, 136
Yamagota, Lieutenant, Japanese 46, 52
Yangtze River 13

Z

Zeblon Field 77, 80, 82, 83, 84, 85, 86, 92, 112, 151
Zimba, John Patrick vii, 7, 13, 148

Printed in Great Britain
by Amazon.co.uk, Ltd.,
Marston Gate.